READING AGAINST RACISM

EDITED BY

Emrys Evans

Open University Press
Buckingham · Philadelphia

Open University Press
Celtic Court
22 Ballmoor
Buckingham
MK18 1XW

and
1900 Frost Road, Suite 101
Bristol, PA 19007, USA

First Published 1992

A catalogue record of this book is available
from the British Library

Library of Congress Cataloging-in-Publication Data

Reading against racism / edited by Emrys Evans.
     p.   cm. – (English, language, and education)
  Includes bibliographical references and index.
  ISBN 0–335–09544–5 (pbk.)
  1. English philology–Study and teaching. 2. Commonwealth of
Nations literature (English)–Study and teaching. 3. Pluralism
(Social sciences) in literature–Study and teaching. 4. Race
relations in literature–Study and teaching. 5. Racism in
literature–Study and teaching. I. Evans, Emrys (W.D. Emrys)
II. Series: English, language, and education series.
PE66.R43   1992
820′.7–dc20   92–16901
                                         CIP

Typeset by Graphicraft Typesetters Limited, Hong Kong
Printed in Great Britain by St Edmundsbury Press,
Bury St Edmunds, Suffolk

READING AGAINST RACISM

Open University Press

English, Language, and Education series

General Editor: Anthony Adams

Lecturer in Education, University of Cambridge

SELECTED TITLES IN THE SERIES

Contents

Pg 33
66
Pg 14

List of contributors

Napheas Akhter (Chapter 8) was born in Azad Kashmir in Pakistan and came to England when she was 4 years old. Neither of her parents spoke English, so that their reliance upon her as an interpreter at a very early age helped her to acquire the English language quickly. As well as English, she speaks and reads Urdu and Panjabi. After taking her first degree in English at Birmingham University, she obtained her Postgraduate Certificate of Education and taught for 1 year in a primary school. She moved to her present post in a large inner-city sixth-form college in 1988.

Rudine Sims Bishop (Chapter 2) is Professor of Education at the Ohio State University. A graduate of West Chester University (Penn.), Professor Bishop also holds a MEd from the University of Pennsylvania and an EdD from Wayne State University in Detroit. She taught elementary school in Pennsylvania for a number of years, and while at Wayne was a participant in the Reading Miscue Research Project. For several years she was on the faculty of the University of Massachusetts, where she directed a graduate level teacher education programme in reading, writing and literature. Professor Bishop is active in the International Reading Association, and has been elected to several positions in the National Council of Teachers of English. She is the author (as Rudine Sims) of *Shadow and Substance: Afro-American Experience in Contemporary Children's Fiction*, published in 1982 by NCTE. Most recently, she has written (as Rudine Sims Bishop) *Presenting Walter Dean Myers*, published in 1990 by Twayne Publications/ G.K. Hall.

Emrys Evans (Editor, Introduction and Chapter 10) was born in North Wales, and brought up bilingual in Welsh and English. An education at Oxford and London Universities ensured the domination of English, but what remains of a second ancient language and its culture is still a valuable resource. He has taught in schools in Gloucester, London and New York, and in colleges and universities in Coventry, Birmingham and Bathurst, New South Wales. He is co-editor of *Readers, Texts, Teachers* (Open

University Press, 1987) and editor of *Young Readers, New Readings* (Hull University Press, 1992). His interests in the teaching of reading and the crossing of cultures come together in two shorter pieces: an article on elements from the Welsh *Mabinogion* in current children's literature (*Children's Literature in Education*, 9(1), 1978) and in 'Children's novels and Welsh mythology, with special reference to the work of Susan Cooper and Alan Garner' (in *The Voice of the Narrator in Children's Literature*, edited by C. Otten and G. Schmidt, The Greenwood Press, 1989).

Jim Kable (Chapters 4 and 11) writes: 'While my name, James Stewart Kable, provides some information about me, I am essentially the product of my family (immediate and extended); of my neighbourhoods; of my education (both formal and informal); of my friends and colleagues; of my New World society in fact. All this is in turn given added meaning by my landscape and by its place in the wider world scene. Like everyone else.

Time spent travelling and living abroad has tempered and refined my perception of the formative phases of my life, as well as confirming, from the accumulated experiences so gained, a concern for the dispossessed, the displaced and for those suffering the discrimination of difference. It is my reading of literature, the eloquent, the understated and the passionate, which clarifies all of these issues best of all.

The years 1991 and 1992 I spent in Japan, teaching English, learning Japanese (culture, history, literature and language), and shall return to Australia in early 1993 to teach Japanese.'

Shahana Mirza (Chapter 5) was born in Leeds, West Yorkshire. Her parents originated from Rabwah, Pakistan, and migrated to Britain in the 1960s. She was brought up in a traditional Muslim environment where education was highly prized. Her studies at the Universities of Leeds and Birmingham enabled her to pursue her interests in language and education. She has since worked in outer-London schools as an English teacher where she has promoted multicultural and anti-racist ideas throughout the mainstream curriculum. She is a member of the Asian Women Writers Collective and has published poetry about racism and cultural diversity. She has also worked as an English/French teacher and equal opportunities co-ordinator at Chessington Community College in Surrey, and is currently employed as a Racial Equality Officer in the London Borough of Hounslow.

Beverley Naidoo (Chapter 7), as a writer of fiction for young people, is the author of *Journey to Jo'burg* (Longman, 1985) (several times referred to in this book) and *Chain of Fire* (Longman, 1991), and is also the author of *Censoring Reality: An Examination of Non-fiction Books on South Africa* (ILEA, 1985). Her doctoral research, from which the material for her chapter is partly drawn, was concerned with exploring issues of racism with white students through literature, the story of a year in an English class where all the literature was written from perspectives strongly indicting racism can be read in *Through Whose Eyes? Exploring Racism: Reader, Text and Context* (Trentham, 1992). Beverley Naidoo is an advisory teacher for cultural diversity in Dorset.

Denise Newfield (Chapter 3) lectures in English Education at the University of the Witwatersrand, Johannesburg, South Africa. In her training of secondary school teachers, she has been concerned to modify the curriculum and methodology of English in order to make it appropriate and relevant to all South Africans. In particular, she has been instrumental in encouraging the teaching of South African literature and media education in the schools. In 1986, she produced an educational video entitled *Teaching Shakespeare through Drama*. In 1988, she co-authored a book on film study called *Chariots of Fire: A Reading*.

Sibani Raychaudhuri (Chapter 6) was born and brought up in Calcutta. After an education in India and Britain, she worked as a teacher in the area of bilingualism and the education of bilingual children in multilingual communities in Britain. At present she is general inspector in a London borough. She writes in both Bengali and English. One of her main concerns is the promotion of the positive aspects of bilingualism and biculturalism. She has published a collection of her own short stories for children in Bengali, *Intabiler Punthi* (Proma, 1987), and has also translated a large number of dual-text books currently used in British schools. She has recently co-edited with Ruth Read an anthology of poetry, *Bengali Poetry – English Poetry* (Kavita, 1990). Sibani Raychaudhuri has been active in many ways, through articles, poems and short stories published in periodicals and anthologies, in promoting South Asian literature and writing by Asian women in Britain.

Lena Strang (Chapters 1 and 9) writes: 'I was born in Ostrobothnia, the Swedish-speaking part of Finland. I grew up as a Swedish/Finnish bilingual, and attended a Swedish medium school. Many members of my family moved to Sweden as migrant workers and have now settled there, forming part of the country's largest minority group.

At university I studied English with the intention of teaching English as a Foreign Language. However, I moved to England, married a British national, and decided to pursue my teaching career here instead. I think my own experiences of migration and adaptation to different cultural situations have proved useful in helping me to appreciate the needs of many pupils in British schools.

In the last fifteen years I have taught English in a number of multi-ethnic secondary schools and colleges in the English West Midlands, and spent one year on teacher exchange in Jamaica. I am now Head of English at Colton Hills School in Wolverhampton.'

Acknowledgements

The editor and the contributors gratefully acknowledge permission from the following publishers for permission to quote from work on which they hold the copyright:

Chapter 5: (Appendix One) © Macdonald & Company (Publishers) Ltd 1987. Reproduced by permission of Simon & Schuster Young Books, Hemel Hempstead, UK.

(Appendix Two) pages from *A Case for Change: Rights, Repression and Responses in South Africa*, published by the Leeds Development Education Centre, 151–153 Cardigan Road, Leeds LS6 1LJ, UK.

(Appendix Three) from *The Child is not Dead*, published by the British Defence and Aid Fund for South Africa, Unit 22, The Ivories, 6–8 Northampton Road, London N1 2HX.

Chapter 6: The English translation of the Tagore poem, 'Railway Station', is taken from *Rabindranath Tagore: Selected Poems*, translated by William Radice (Penguin Books, 1985). Translation, Introduction, Notes and Glossary © William Radice 1985. Reproduced by permission of Penguin Books Ltd. Every effort has been made to contact the publishers of the original Bengali text.

The editor also wishes to acknowledge the support of the BRITE (Binlingualism and its Role in the Teaching of English) Project, funded by the University Grants Committee at the University of Birmingham, in the completion of this volume, and to thank Brenda Cox for her constant help in the correspondence, typing and word-processing involved.

General editor's introduction

Approaches to multicultural education in a number of English-speaking countries have undergone a series of changes in prevailing attitudes. Few, if any, in English-speaking countries, would currently argue for a simplistic policy of assimilation of students from ethnic minority backgrounds, even though such policies are still not unknown in mainland Europe, but many uncertainties remain about what practical principles should inform our policies.

So far as England and Wales are concerned, the last major public statement on the issue, the 1985 Swann Report, *Education for All* (London: HMSO) seems to have guided much of the thinking behind the Report of the Cox Working Group on the National Curriculum, *English for Ages 5 to 16* (London: DES). Both share a possible limitation in their failure to recognize sufficiently the positive values involved in having bilingual, or multilingual, pupils in classrooms, and Cox explicitly quotes Swann in arguing for a seeming centrality of English so far as language is concerned:

> We believe that all children should be entitled to obtain a full command of the English language, both spoken and written. Otherwise they will be disadvantaged, not only in their study of other subjects, but also in their working life. We note that in this respect we are following the path already trodden by the Swann Committee. They stated firmly, '. . . the key to equality of opportunity, to academic success and, more broadly, to participation on equal terms as a full member of society, is good command of English and the emphasis must therefore we feel be on the learning of English.' The Swann Committee had also noted, '. . . the views expressed very clearly to us at our various meetings with parents from the whole range of ethnic minority groups that they want and indeed expect the education system to give their children above all a good command of English as rapidly as possible'.
>
> (Cox Report, para. 10.5)

While this is fair enough so far as it goes, and no-one would deny the vital importance of access to English for all our citizens, there is also a danger of a marginalization of the language and culture of ethnic minority groups, a danger for which Swann was much criticized in some quarters on its publication.

Interestingly enough, however, Cox also goes much further in insisting upon the importance of including in the National Curriculum the study of literature in English from other cultures and other parts of the English-speaking world. This provides a useful starting point for the focus of the papers in the present collection, even though it has been argued that Cox's own strong advocacy of this has been somewhat muted in the actual pre-scriptions of the National Curriculum as promulgated in the Secretary of State's Orders in Council.

None the less, literature from sources outside the traditional English culture is now firmly on the agenda in our schools, alongside two powerful alternatives to the integrationist model for multicultural education. The first of these is an increasing emphasis upon education for life in a pluralist society, a strong advocacy of the positive values of celebrating diversity within a pluralist society. The second is the recognition that, within this pluralism, there is still a great deal of prejudice and intolerance of which education, if it is to be genuinely concerned with equality of opportunity for all, must take account. Hence the rise in the concern for anti-racist edu-cation. A possible problem with this is, however, the feeling that by its very nature 'anti-racist' education has to be somewhat negative; making people feel guilty for the racism of their own attitudes and those of people around them. This was certainly true of much of the original movement towards anti-racist education in schools, a good deal of which had a strongly felt political ideology at its heart. While many of us might share this ideology, it remains the case that a more positive approach to the issue would be welcome and move it away from the danger of sloganizing and propaganda, even in the best of causes.

The present collection provides just such an opportunity. In drawing, in its various chapters, upon a number of different traditions, it shows some of the ways in which the recommendations of the Cox Working Group can be put into practice and the ways in which reading and literature can serve as a basis for a more positive approach to anti-racist education. In that it draws widely on authoritative authors from the world scene, it should provide useful material for cultural and literary comparisons that will inform the thinking and practice of teachers throughout the international community of English teaching. This seems important. If we are to practise the ideals of anti-racist education, we need to be more aware of what is happening outside the boundaries of our own shores, wherever these may be. There is still, necessarily, too much parochialism in the experience of most teachers of the teaching of their subject. In the case of a subject such as English, with its worldwide constituency and concerns, this is especially to be regretted.

Emrys Evans's collection is to be recommended not only because of the excellence of the essays that it contains, but also on the basis of the enterprise as a whole. In its consistent advocacy of a positive approach to the challenges of anti-racist education and its celebration of the role of literature in this context, it breaks new ground in its thinking and provides a beginning for committed classroom work that will take us far beyond the muted liberalism of Swann and its offshoots.

Anthony Adams

Introduction

EMRYS EVANS

This book is about the reading and teaching of literature and its relationship to differences of race and culture in English-speaking countries. The 'mechanical' aspects of learning to read – as well as the deeper psychological and physiological features indicated by recent writers (e.g. Smith, 1978; Goodman, 1982) – are not our primary concern. When readers reach the stage at which novels, plays and poems are able to affect their cultural presuppositions in matters like class, gender and race, these mechanics must already be working quite well.

It is consistent with the general use of the terms 'reading' and 'readers' in this series that we should refer mainly to *literary* reading. The emphasis is on what Louise Rosenblatt (1978) calls 'aesthetic' rather than 'efferent' reading. In other words, we are concerned with reading that is, on the whole, an end in itself; where, as Rosenblatt puts it, 'the reader's primary concern is with what happens *during* the actual reading event', rather than when 'the reader's attention is focussed primarily on what will remain as residue *after* the reading' (pp. 23 and 24, original emphases).

We are also very much concerned about the world where our pupils and students live and where their reading occurs, both the microcosms of school and home and the macrocosm of political change, shifting populations, and different people's perceptions of each other. All of these things are also, of course, the stuff of literature. And 'Racism', the final word of our title, is one of those phenomena which threaten the peace of our world, and which novels, plays and poems reflect and question. Undoubtedly there is room for other collections, more or less like this one, which will examine the relationship between literature, education, and gender, class, wealth or political views. Ultimately, such books might perhaps be summarized in a single volume with a more positive title, like 'Reading for Tolerance' or 'Reading for Inquiry'. In such a field, this volume is meant as one – and we hope useful – contribution.

There is now an increasing consciousness among a wider public that the field of literary reading in English is widening. We see clear evidence of this in the UK in the recurrent references which appear in the government document *English for Ages 5 to 16* (DES, 1989), which forms the foundation for the new National Curriculum in English. (Like many such documents in Britain, this report is usually briefly referred to as the Cox Report, after Professor C.B. Cox, who chaired the committee which produced it. We shall follow this practice here.) An awareness of the same need to broaden our view of what constitutes literature for study is evident in other English-speaking countries. This will appear in several of the chapters in this book, but one public acknowledgement of the fact in the USA was the appearance of NCTE's *English Journal*, 79(8) for December 1990, subtitled 'A global perspective'. It shows how novels and stories from the Soviet Union, China, Liberia and South Africa, among other countries, have found their place in the curricula of American schools today.

In the Cox Report's recommendations for Attainment Targets in Reading – one of the three major areas to be taught and assessed in English, along with Talking and Writing – from their Level 7 upwards (i.e. from about ages 13 to 16), there is a recurring insistence on the reading of 'works from different cultures'. And later, in chapter seven of the report, 'Literature', the following paragraph appears:

> Today, literature in English in the classroom can – and should – be drawn from different countries. All pupils need to be aware of the richness of experience offered by such writing, so that they may be introduced to the ideas and feelings of cultures different from their own. English teachers should seek opportunities to exploit the multicultural aspects of literature. Novels from India or Caribbean poetry might be used for study of differing cultural perspectives, for example. Not only should this lead to a broader awareness of a greater range of human 'thought and feeling', but – through looking at literature from different parts of the world and written from different points of view – pupils should also be in a position to gain a better understanding of the cultural heritage of English literature itself.
>
> (DES, 1989)

Our title, *Reading Against Racism*, presupposes this broader awareness which Cox requires. Later chapters will recommend and discuss the use of novels, poems and plays written in the Indian subcontinent, South Africa, the Caribbean, the USA and other countries.

It may not, however, be obvious how the reading of a novel, a play or a poem can actually be *for* or *against* anything. Here we have to start, I think, from Louise Rosenblatt's (1978) point of view that 'a text, once it leaves its author's hands, is simply paper and ink until a reader evokes from it a literary work'. Salman Rushdie (1990b) takes this idea a stage further in his Herbert Read Memorial Lecture, 'Is nothing sacred?'. 'What is forged', he says, 'in the secret act of reading, is a different kind of identity, as the reader and the writer merge, through the medium of the text, to become a collective being that both writes as it reads and reads as it writes, and creates, jointly, that unique work, "their" novel'. With other colleagues, I have tried to argue elsewhere (Corcoran and Evans, 1987) that to educate the skills needed by a reader to enable him or her to reach out to the author and to establish this 'secret identity' is the business of literature teachers. Wolfgang Iser (1978) speaks of how 'author and reader are to share the game of the imagination', and I have tried to develop this idea, by suggesting that 'the teacher's object all the time, whether working with very young children, older students advancing in their appreciation of literature, or even adults who have returned to evening or day classes in the hope of improving their knowledge and enjoyment of poetry, novels, and drama, is to make it possible for them to play this game as well as possible. And the object of the game itself is not to win – there is no way of winning – but to make the experience as rich as possible each time one plays' (Corcoran and Evans, 1987: 31).

Racism is one of many attitudes which may be suggested, confirmed, questioned or modified in the experience of each of us, either through our non-literary lives or through our reading. In the one case we will read newspapers, watch television, go shopping, attend school and meet people in our homes or in the street. The people we listen to or talk with, the faces we see around us, the views of our friends and family and the utterances of preachers, politicians and commentators affect our feelings and thoughts from day to day. All the information and all the opinions we receive and form from these sources are part of what we bring to our encounter, through the pages of a book, with the writers of the novels, plays and poems we read. The writers reach out to us, through their texts, with their efforts to offer us further, more strongly distilled, images and experiences for us to interpret.

Literary texts themselves can contain references to race, as to gender, class, attitudes to the environment and many other controversial issues. These references may be neutral, inflammatory, sceptical or healing. How readers meet these attitudes depends on their experience of literary reading, and part (an important part, one would hope) of that experience will be the way they have encountered literature at school, at college or at university. Entirely uneducated readers are likely to meet the text naively, failing to distinguish opinion from fact, insensitive to irony, satire and ambiguity, and ready to be swayed by any presuppositions the text seems to offer. Readers educated in the ways we try to propose here will bring varying degrees of scepticism and sophistication to bear on their reading, so that in the end their own personal experience, whether of the world or of books, can help them to analyse, question and interrogate the text.

We have made no attempt to define 'racism' here. It is a complex and complicated idea, and indeed it is possible, perhaps desirable, that the term will lose its usefulness before long. However, along with certain cultural prejudices, economic assumptions and educational myths, the idea of mankind's being divided into different races has often collected associations with those races having different religions. To publish this collection in the UK in the 1990s with no acknowledgement of the so-called 'Rushdie affair' would be to bury our heads in the sand. It is a controversy which concerns both religious belief and one's attitude to the role of literature. It has resulted in violent confrontations between those who read Rushdie's novel, *The Satanic Verses*, in one way, and those who read it in another. One of the ways, I believe, is the way we are advocating here, and that is the way in which Rushdie himself has defended his work. As he himself puts it (Rushdie, 1990a):

> Human beings understand themselves and shape their futures by arguing and challenging and questioning and saying the unsayable; not by bowing the knee, whether to gods or to men.

The other way is the way of Religions of the Book. If a book is believed to the word of a god, brought to the world by the inspiration of a prophet, then the words of that book become immutable and, in the view of those who read it with that assumption, the book stands to its reader in an entirely different relationship from the one we are proposing for literary works. Until the objections of British and other Muslims to Rushdie's writing, and the pronouncement of the *fatwa* by the Ayatollah Khomeini with its subsequent renewals, I do not think most of us would have believed that a novel could have been read in this way – though there have been examples of similar clashes between literary texts and the views of some Christian fundamentalist believers.

The rest of this book is divided into two main sections. In the first of these, 'Contexts', the writers set out to show, in different ways, how four basically English-speaking societies are affected by a history of cultural and racial diversity. Lena Strang says something about the position of the children of immigrants from the Indian subcontinent in British schools; Rudine Sims Bishop recommends Afro-American books for children; Denise Newfield gives us a view of the rapidly changing situation in the literature classrooms of South Africa; and Jim Kable, through an autobiographical account of his own personal development as a teacher, shows how the mixture of cultures affects Australian society and its literature.

In the second section, 'Case Studies', the majority of the examples are from the UK. Shahana Mirza has introduced year 8 students in South London to Beverley Naidoo's *Journey to Jo'Burg*; Sibani Raychaudhuri compares Bengali and English poetry with students and teachers. Beverley Naidoo (as teacher and writer here, rather than as novelist) shows how questions of discrimination in the Deep South of the USA can be brought to life for English south-coast children, and Lena Strang demonstrates the effectiveness of a programme for inner-city adolescents involving contact with younger children. Napheas Akhter finds poetry enlivening and linguistically valuable in a class of second-language English students, and the editor's case study suggests that overseas English literature can widen the awareness of an 'all-white' group of students in a quiet country town. Finally, we return to Australia for Jim Kable's account of using Australian 'immigrant' literature with adult students in New South Wales.

All these viewpoints are consistent with a basic view, of which two aspects are important. The first is that two kinds of knowledge are essential to the more sophisticated and sceptical reading we advocate: self-knowledge and knowledge of the changing society we live in. Jim Kable argues forcefully that teachers need first to examine the nurseries, schools and colleges of their own presuppositions. So he ranges back over the history of his own family, before and since its establishment in Australia; the nature of the community he grew up in, and his own experience as an adult and a teacher. Most of us have not set out to review our experience so fully, but each has contributed a short biographical note in which these aspects of our histories are touched on.

The fact that we can all claim some record of bilingualism, multi-culturalism, or personal experience of migration or cultural transplantation does not, I believe, make us peculiar. Very few individuals could examine their own backgrounds, as Jim Kable does, without finding some evidence of a complexity of origin some time within the past four or five generations.

Yet there seems in some human beings still to be a strange desire for that fictitious homogeneity of culture which is dangerously referred to as 'purity'. The terms favoured by Nazism continue to haunt us, and only the awareness of this tendency which has been fostered by writers like George Steiner and Primo Levi can help us avoid it. In Jim Kable's approach to his mixed classes in New South Wales, with their origins spread all over Europe and Asia, as well as the Koori children of indigenous Australians, and in Lena Strang's invitation to her students from homes in Birmingham, where the mother-tongue was Panjabi, Kashmiri or Bengali, to value their own cultures and to pass them on to younger children through their own writing, we see self-knowledge explored.

In Rudine Sims Bishop's evaluation of Black children's literature from Europe and North America, Beverley Naidoo's use of a Black American novel in the south of England, and Sibani Raychaudhuri's paralleling of English and Bengali poetry, we see the enhancement of knowledge about, and vicarious experience of, the breadth of human experience available to us. Until quite recently, we have accepted the absurdity of examination syllabuses in English literature, not only in the UK, but in Australia and even in countries like Zimbabwe and Uganda, which were confined to the study of 'classic' English writers – Austen, Dickens, Shakespeare, Words-worth. There is no need to decry the study of these authors – they are an im-portant part of the literary culture of all readers in English, whether as a first or a second language, inherit – in order to encourage the reading and study of writers like Achebe, Ngugi, Narayan, Desai, Naipaul and Brathwaite.

It does not on the whole seem to us helpful that many writers about literature and race confine themselves primarily to the exclusion of texts whose
attitudes they condemn. So, in the field of children's literature, Hugh
Lofting has been censured for his portrait of Prince Bumppo, Enid Blyton
for her tendency to xenophobia and her middle-class myopia, and *Little
Black Sambo* for its derogatory picture of a black child. In adult and classical
literature, Shakespeare has been criticized for his presentation of Shylock
and Othello, and Conrad (by Chinua Achebe) for his view of black Africans
in *Heart of Darkness*.

If we are able to foster the kind of self-knowledge and awareness of
cultural diversity I have tried to describe, however, such censorship would
not be necessary. It would be the proper achievement of a 'reading against . . .'
policy that it did not need to protect its students from even the most overtly
racist material, because they would be able to approach it critically and
analytically, and so not fall victim to its unexamined or deliberately insidious
assumptions.

There is, for example, a passage in Dickens's *Our Mutual Friend* which
might offend modern opinion. Richard Wilfer (R.W.), a poor but cheerful
city clerk, has been given a new suit of clothes by his elder daughter, who
has unexpectedly found herself with money to offer him. He is talking to Mr
Rokesmith, the mysterious central character who knows them both:

'I don't know whether you happen to have read many books of African Travel,
Mr Rokesmith?' said R.W.
'I have read several.'
'Well, you know, there's usually a King George, or a King Boy, or a King
Sambo, or a King Bill, or Bull, or Rum, or Junk, or whatever name the sailors
may have happened to give him.'
'Where?' asked Rokesmith.
'Anywhere. Anywhere in Africa, I mean. Pretty well everywhere, I may say;
for black kings are cheap – and I think' – said R.W., with an apologetic air, 'nasty.'
'I am much of your opinion, Mr Wilfer. You were going to say – ?'
'I was going to say, the king is generally dressed in a London hat only, or a
Manchester pair of braces, or one epaulette, or a uniform coat, with his legs in
the sleeves, or something of that kind.'
'Just so,' said the Secretary.
'In confidence, I assure you, Mr Rokesmith,' observed the cheerful cherub,
'that when more of my family were at home and to be provided for, I used to
remind myself immensely of that king.'

Of course, one can see immediately how such a passage would offend an
African of the present day, or any black person, who read it. Yet literature is
scattered with such references, made by persons who would have regarded
themselves as belonging to the majority in the culture at the time and place
when the book was written, to minorities around them. And this is one kind
of passage that an education for reading against racism should help us to

read. We should find ourselves able to look for all its contexts, among which are its historical context, and its context in the novel as a whole. R.W. derives his picture of African kings from the only sources available to him – the travellers' tales he thinks Rokesmith may also have read. He uses them, not deliberately to belittle Africans or their leaders, but to invite a laugh against himself, in the days when his family demanded expense far beyond his modest means, and he had to live in patchwork clothing.

The context of the novel as a whole, attacking as it does the complacency of the Victorian middle classes, and sympathizing with the plight of the poor while violently criticizing the injustices of the Poor Law, might also suggest how improbable a deliberate racist slur, in twentieth-century terms, would be. The passage I have chosen to quote is no high point in the rich texture of *Our Mutual Friend*. In fact, when I met it recently on a second reading, I had quite forgotten it existed. But there it is: it can be read fairly, or it can be read unfairly. We wish to argue here for, and to exemplify some practical approaches to, a generally fairer and richer reading of literature.

A second basic viewpoint shared, I believe, by all the contributors to this collection is that, for reading to play an effective part in increasing knowledge and awareness and so reducing the tensions that racism now causes, the process must be given time to run deep and to penetrate consciousness fully. There has been some evidence in recent years that the hasty deployment of deliberate anti-racist or multiracial programmes in schools is not always effective, and can even prove counterproductive, underlining differences without establishing how difference itself can be rewarding.

Teachers who read Jim Kable's account of his own growth in awareness, and his increasing ability to apply this awareness energetically to arousing a similar self-awareness in his students, will find an invitation to examine their own experience and their present stance. Denise Newfield's record of a society in sometimes violent transition, needing to learn – across the artificially heightened barriers of race and custom – about each other's experiences as recorded in poetry, novels and short stories, may at first feel thankful that their own societies seem more stable. Second thoughts, however, will invite us all to profit from South Africa's experience, as well as to look for ways to help that society in its development. Similarly, each chapter here, whether it ranges widely over a broad question or suggests practical ways of bringing discussions and redirection into our classrooms, advocates thought, organized application, sensitivity, and the broadening and increasing responsiveness of our own and our students' reading.

References

Corcoran, B. and Evans, E. (1987). *Readers, Texts, Teachers*. Milton Keynes: Open University Press.

Department of Education and Science (1989). *English for Ages 5 to 16* (The Cox Report). London: DES and the Welsh Office.

Goodman, K.S. (1982). In Gollasch, F. (ed.), *Language and Literacy: The Collected Writings of Kenneth S. Goodman*, Vols 1 and 2. London: Routledge and Kegan Paul.

Iser, W. (1978). *The Act of Reading*. Baltimore: Johns Hopkins University Press/ London: Routledge and Kegan Paul.

National Council for the Teaching of English (1990). A global perspective. *The English Journal*, 79(8): 16–28.

Rosenblatt, L. (1978). *The Reader, The Text, The Poem*. Carbondale, Ill.: Southern Illinois University Press.

Rushdie, S. (1990a). *In Good Faith*. Cambridge: Granta.

Rushdie, S. (1990b). *Is Nothing Sacred?* The Herbert Read Memorial Lecture, 6 February 1990. Cambridge: Granta.

(Both these texts are now available in: Rushdie, S. (1991). *Imaginary Homelands: Essays and Criticism 1981–1991*. Cambridge: Granta.)

Smith, F. (1978). *Reading*. Cambridge: Cambridge University Press.

PART ONE

Contexts

1 Language against racism in the UK: The classroom as a multilingual publishing house

LENA STRANG

The development of my own practice in several inner-city multiracial schools has taken place over a number of years. I think my position as a Finnish-Swedish bilingual[1]* who has lived in Britain for several years has helped me appreciate the complexities of the situation that many pupils face. The responses made have often been pragmatic, sometimes based on 'hunches' of what works in the classroom, but much of the practice has been informed by a process of 'osmosis'. By this I mean absorbing the steady flow of literature and accounts of good practice, particularly from ILEA (Inner London Education Authority), together with working in a collegial atmosphere in innovative departments where reflection on practice takes place. Working with examination syllabuses that have allowed us to design and moderate our own courses, and the increased element of assessed course work in British examinations generally, have meant a shift from the sterile notion of 'preparing pupils for exams' to validating the activities that go on in the day-to-day classroom. In this chapter, I will try to address some of the issues involved in teaching in a multiracial situation. In Chapter 9, I will attempt to place practical classroom work in this context.

The language environment of Asian students in inner-city schools is a particularly complex one. According to Taylor and Hegarty (1985), the linguistic experience of Asian students can vary enormously. A few may be semilingual, many are bilingual and others multilingual. Many may also be literate in more than one language. There has long been a reluctance in the UK to accept such varied linguistic experience. Taylor and Hegarty (1985: 145) see it as imperative for 'educators to make clear whether they see such skills as enriching assets, disadvantageous handicaps or even deficiencies requiring treatment'.

* Superscript numerals refer to numbered notes at the end of each chapter.

Indeed, this varied linguistic experience is too often seen as an obstacle to a child's learning and the problem is located within some deficiency in the child or his or her background. Dittmar (1976: 94) charts the Bernstein-Labov debate and dismantles the premise on which remediation programmes are built:

> The assumptions of the Deficit Hypothesis have enormous implications for educational methods in schools. By implying that children have no language at all (an implication based on the result from inappropriate test situations) and in connection with this by demanding speech drills in the standard language as compensation, they have labelled the first acquired language of the child as dysfunctional and bad.

These assumptions about the child lead to certain teaching approaches which see the need to replace the child's own language with forms of standard English. According to Chatwin (1984), these measures frequently include 'correcting "faulty" usage in pupils' speech – particularly "slovenly" speech and "slang" and the "broken" English of some black pupils'. In some instances, elocution lessons or speech therapy might be thought necessary as an attempt to correct faulty usage of language. Since languages other than English are thought to hinder acquisition of English, their use would be discouraged. In written work, all non-standard forms would be corrected as signs of laziness or carelessness. Many of the tasks presented would be undemanding and would consist of 'busy work' – children occupied in often meaningless chores such as copying notes or filling in boxes – frequently as a means of exercising classroom control. Students would also be presented with models of 'good' literature by established English authors. Often, 'self-fulfilling prophecies' are at work; the perceived inadequacies in the child do indeed lead to expected failure.

Stubbs (1980) distinguishes between the terms 'deprivation' and 'disadvantage'. He sees 'deprivation' as implying an inherent deficiency within the child, whereas 'disadvantage' concentrates on the social experience which 'disadvantages' the child in terms of what the school considers desirable. He presents a 'difference theory' and suggests that 'it is cultural and linguistic differences which cause problems' (p. 148). A version of this theory (cf. Labov) holds that it is not the differences themselves which cause the problems; rather, it is the way these differences are interpreted by teachers which is problematic.

George Keith (1988: 138), who helped to pioneer new approaches to 'A' level English Language studies in Britain, acknowledges the serious implications these notions still have on classroom practice:

> The Bernstein-Labov debate, of what now seems another age, highlighted the fact that what may be perceived as differences in the outside world are perceived within school as deficiencies. No doubt it is easier to teach in terms of deficit theory but the habit of doing so has led to more problems rather than fewer.

It is clear that this view of the Asian or black child is not very helpful. It is often accompanied with stereotypical notions of, for instance, the black child who is good at sport or music and the Asian child who is conformist or religious. What is taught in schools is equally important. The curriculum itself can be a powerful vehicle for perpetuating racism. An ethnocentric perspective can through distortion and omission lead to misrepresentation of people's historical and cultural experiences (Gundara *et al.*, 1986).

This view of the language curriculum is racist because it is fundamentally *exclusionary*. It excludes the child's own experience and does not seize the opportunities presented to make classrooms into rich learning environments where students from diverse cultural, racial and linguistic groups can learn together. It is very disturbing that this attitude seems to be perpetuated in the 'Bilingual Children' chapter of the Cox Report (DES, 1989) and the resulting sections of the English National Curriculum.

However, the distinction between multicultural and anti-racist education is not very useful either. Some critics (e.g. Mullard, 1983) see multicultural education as being primarily concerned with content, with an emphasis on 'tokenistic' celebrations of diversity which do not challenge the fundamental racist structures in education. I find the position of Grinter (1985) more workable. He suggests that multicultural and anti-racist education are 'part of a combined strategy'. It would be counterproductive to reject the development of a multicultural curriculum and hence alienate potential allies who are genuinely working for the anti-racist cause. They should not be seen as alternative approaches; liberal multicultural education could arguably be part of the overall anti-racist strategy which poses a challenge to institutional racism.

'Inclusionary' education

The criteria by which the education of children in multiracial schools should be measured is that of *inclusion*. We need to ask where the bilingual child is represented in the curriculum in the same way as we need to ask where girls and working-class children feature. Bilingual children need to be included in mainstream schooling in order to have full and equal access to the curriculum. As I have argued elsewhere (Strang, 1983), there is now much evidence which points to the racist implications of separate educational provision, particularly remedial and language-withdrawal provision.

The pupil with 'no language' is a fallacy. Children, particularly in multilingual classrooms, have considerable linguistic knowledge. A survey of languages and dialects spoken in London schools (Rosen and Burgess, 1980) came up with 55 languages and 24 overseas-based dialects. Acknowledging and using linguistic diversity within the classroom may be central to enhancing students' achievements and combating racism and prejudice generally.

There has been much controversy regarding the question of the language of Afro-Caribbean children and to what extent negative attitudes towards language contribute towards educational underachievement (Coard, 1971; Edwards, 1979; DES, 1981; Sutcliffe, 1982). The outcome of the 'black English' case in Ann Arbor, Michigan, is an important milestone. The suit brought against the school by black students and parents charged that teachers who were ignorant of the structures of black English and insisted on constant correction of children's speech 'were undermining the confidence of children accustomed to "black English" and were making it difficult for the students to learn to read English correctly' (Peterson, 1979). As a result of the ruling, teachers, were asked to attend courses to aid their understanding of 'black English', so that they could accommodate it in their teaching. The School Board subsequently reported improved attitudes and attendance by students, although they could not quantify any improvements in reading levels.

In Britain, there have been many attempts to adopt the conscious use and enjoyment of dialect as part of classroom work. Richmond (1979a,b) discusses his work with Afro-Caribbean pupils and points to the way acknowledgement of their language leads to enchanced self-perception and performance.

The Black Ink Collective is a community publishing group whose first published work was based on students' writing in South London schools. Hoyle (1983) describes work with young black students and explains that 'the idea was to tap the real interests of the children and to produce materials that they could identify with and be proud of'. This resulted in a magazine, *Brixton's Baddest Magazine*, which drew on children's own stories and poetry. In turn, this led to the production of other materials such as an ABC colouring book featuring Natty Dread and a series of other stories with the same character. Hoyle maintains that these stories played a role in raising the standards of poor readers.

In the secondary stage, writing may become a rather pointless activity and often the only purpose for a piece of writing is that the teacher has requested it. However, the importance of getting away from the artificiality of writing and providing real purposes and real audiences has increasingly been recognized. The publishing of children's work is not a new notion. Worpole (1977: 187) argues that 'we have the technological potential now to abolish completely the traditional distinction between writers and readers (producers and consumers), providing we ourselves are prepared to re-think our notion of literary production'.

Literature: 'Good' or 'bad'?

According to Jeffcoate (1982), much of children's literature tends to portray minorities in a harmful and demeaning manner. It ignores working-class experience or presents a view that is either a travesty or a caricature. It frequently confines females to subordinate and stereotypical roles such as the weak and unenterprising little girl. It also omits the experience of black and other ethnic minorities; or, where it represents them, they are often seen in ethnocentric or even racist terms. Milner (1975) has tried to demonstrate the harmful effects negative stereotyping has on children. According to Jeffcoate, while it is difficult to quantify this, there is evidence which points to *positive* changes in attitudes and attainment among children when books containing racist and sexist stereotypes have been replaced by books which offer positive images. Jeffcoate (1982: 27) concludes that 'books *can* make a difference . . . can be an effective tool in reducing racism and sexism in society'.

However, the notion of using evaluative criteria to judge chidren's literature is rather crude. Originally, checklists were used by librarians and teachers to select book boxes for classroom use, so as to avoid the cruder forms of bias (see, e.g. Klein, 1982). It is not very useful to use this yardstick when approaching literature generally. It may be of more help to consider bias in connection with fluent reader behaviour. We should try to develop effective readers who can cope not only with the literal meaning of the text, but who can also read between and beyond the lines. Fluent readers become critical, discerning readers. I agree with Moore (1989: 25) that, 'Our ultimate aim is to educate children to become aware, critical and perceptive readers, who know what makes a good book, and who can recognize and reject "bad" books for themselves.'

It is also important to challenge the notion of what constitutes 'good' literature, worthy of inclusion in our syllabuses. I find the arguments of Eagleton (1983: 11) helpful here. He contends that 'the so-called "literary canon", the unquestioned "great tradition" of the "national literature", has to be recognized as a *construct*, fashioned by particular people for particular reasons at a certain time'.

The 'A' level literature course offered at the college where I taught recently has a multicultural focus and, apart from more traditional authors, it also incorporates Asian and Afro-Caribbean authors. As part of the students' initial background reading to the course, they were asked to read a collection of contemporary *Short Stories from India, Pakistan and Bangladesh* (Ash, 1980). It was instructive to note their reactions. Apart from two dissenting voices – one who thought stories of this kind could lead to divisions between racial groups in the class and another who thought 'A' level literature was about English, not Asian literature? – the consensus was positive:

> It was very interesting reading matter and would, I think in many cases, remove the barrier between races. For Asians all we get in school is Shakespeare and how great he was. What about our Asian authors and stories? Is this a truly multicultural society?
>
> (Kaliq)

When first introduced to this book I thought it would be another boring Indian fairy book! However, it turned out to be a most interesting group of tales from the modern Indian subcontinent and a good choice for background reading to an 'A' level syllabus. The stories helped create lively discussions in our group and made us think about cultures and societies other than our own.

(Anthony)

I think an anti-racist approach encourages reflection on practice. It is an appreciation that children themselves must engage actively with the business of learning. They are not vacant and passive recipients of knowledge; they are invited to share in the process of learning. 'When teachers demystify the means of learning and make it explicit to learners what the processes are, then both parties in education are actively participating; the student needs to be as personally engaged as the teacher if the learning is to be successful' (Torbe and Medway, 1981). Children should be encouraged to look upon themselves as active 'meaning makers' (Britton, 1982) who can handle language and control words rather than be on the receiving end. Explorations with and into language could then be seen as children making and preserving meanings for themselves.

Finally, the key factor which we should not lose sight of is whether the education we provide enhances attainment. I am not referring to the limited instrumental view of schooling concerned with 'basic skills', i.e. drilling, testing and scores. Examinations do not have to be the traditional straitjackets where anxieties of 'covering the syllabus' have stultifying effects on the process of learning. In the English classroom in particular, much worthwhile work has gone on in Britain under the auspices of 'Mode 3', where teachers design and moderate their own examination course. At 'A' level, there are 'alternative' Literature courses on offer where teachers and students can decide on their own focus. 'A' level Language gives students the opportunity to undertake their own action research into varieties of language use. I also think that the General Certificate of Secondary Education (GCSE) can have enabling effects. It is an inclusionary examination intended for 95 per cent of pupils. Despite initial difficulties, the examination is proving successful. According to DES (1988: 3):

> There have been considerable improvements in the quality of teaching and learning . . . The GCSE has increased the pupils' motivation; helped to raise teachers' expectations; enriched subjects of the curriculum . . . The increased requirements of assessed course work have helped to raise levels of performance and provide a fairer system of assessment.

The report is strongly critical of the alternative courses (e.g. the prevocational education courses) 'low-attaining' pupils are frequently directed to. These are not seen as being 'in the best interests of pupils' but are 'encouraging a narrow range of learning'. I am not going to be drawn into this area of debate, which in itself would require a separate chapter, but I would like to draw parallels between the new 'initiatives' that have proliferated in secondary schools in the last few years – providing a diluted and heavily behaviouristic skills-oriented curriculum – and compensatory education which denies equal access to the curriculum by many (often ethnic minority) pupils. However, I think increased attainment goes hand in hand with encouraging pupils to develop the less tangible and difficult-to-measure qualities of increased confidence and self-esteem, together with a critical awareness of their own position and that of others in society.

This is best illustrated by a comment made by Fardous, a sixth-form Asian student who completed a 2-year 'A' level Literature course at college. Her commentary is part of a section in our *Student Course Handbook*:

> The multicultural aspect has led me to challenge many stereotypes held by society and my own perception of India, the problems confronted by Asian people living in Britain and the position of women within Asian social structure . . . English Literature has not only been the most enjoyable of my 'A' level courses, but also the one which I feel, has ultimately educated me the most.

Fardous also gained a good grade in her examination and went on to study at university.

Note

1 Readers who are interested in the intricate linguistic and social situation faced by Swedish- and Finnish-speaking Finns, particularly 'immigrants' in Sweden, should consult Skutnabb-Kangas (1981).

References

Ash, R. (1980). *Short Stories from India, Pakistan and Bangladesh*. London: Harrap.
Britton, J. (1982). *Prospect and Retrospect: Selected Essays of James Britton* (edited by G. Pradl). London: Heinemann Educational.
Chatwin, R. (1984). Language in the multicultural classroom: Some practical strategies. *Multicultural Education Review*, No. 2, Spring: 5.
Coard, B. (1971). *How the West Indian Child is made Educationally Subnormal in British Classrooms*. London: New Beacon Books.
Department of Education and Science (1981). *West Indian Children in our Schools* (The Rampton Report). London: HMSO.
Department of Education and Science (1988). *The Introduction of the General Certificate of Secondary Education in Schools 1986–88*. London: HMSO.
Department of Education and Science (1989). *English for Ages 5 to 16* (The Cox Report). London: DES and the Welsh Office.
Dittmar, N. (1976). *Sociolinguistics: A Critical Survey of Theory and Application*. London: Edward Arnold.
Eagleton, T. (1983). *Literary Theory: An Introduction*. Oxford: Basil Blackwell.
Edwards, V.K. (1979). *The West Indian Language Issue in British Schools*. London: Routledge and Kegan Paul.
Grinter, R. (1985). Bridging the gulf: The need for anti-racist multicultural education. *Multicultural Teaching*, 3(2), Spring: 12.

Gundara, J., Jones, C. and Kimberley, K. (1986). *Racism, Diversity and Education*. London: Hodder and Stoughton.

Hoyle, S. (1983). Self-made materials. *Education Journal*, 1(1), January: 20.

Hoyles, M. (ed.) (1977). *The Politics of Literacy*. London: Writers and Readers Publishing Cooperative.

Jeffcoate, R. (1982). Social values in children's books. In *Children, Language and Literature*. Milton Keynes: Open University Press.

Keith, G. (1988). Variety, more than the spice of language. In *Learning Me Your Language*. London: Mary Glasgow Publications.

Klein, G. (1982). *Resources for Multicultural Education: An Introduction*. London: Longman.

Marenbon, J. (1987). *English our English*. London: Centre for Policy Studies.

Milner, D. (1975). *Children and Race*. Harmondsworth: Penguin.

Moore, B. (1989). The 'bad book box': Racial bias and stereotype in children's books. *Multicultural Teaching*, 7(2), Spring: 23.

Mullard, C. (1983). The racial code: Its features, rules and change. In Barton, L. and Walker, S. (eds), *Race, Class and Education*. London: Croom Helm.

Peterson, I. (1979). Limited gains found with 'Black English'. *The New York Times*, 12 June.

Richmond, J. (1979a). Dialect features in mainstream writing. *Multiracial Education*, 8, Autumn: 6.

Richmond, J. (1979b). Dialect in the classroom. *The English Magazine*, No. 2, Autumn.

Rosen, H. and Burgess, T. (1980). *Languages and Dialects of London School Children: An Investigation*. London: Ward Lock Educational.

Skutnabb-Kangas, T. (1981). *Bilingualism or Not: The Education of Minorities*. Bristol: Multilingual Matters.

Smith, F. (1982). *Reading*. Cambridge: Cambridge University Press.

Strang, L. (1983). 'A critical analysis of provisions made for meeting the language needs of English as a Second Language (ESL) learners in an inner-ring secondary school.' Unpublished MEd dissertation, University of Birmingham.

Stubbs, M. (1980). *Language and Literacy: The Sociolinguistics of Reading and Writing*. London: Routledge and Kegan Paul.

Sutcliffe, D. (1982). *British Black English*. Oxford: Basil Blackwell.

Taylor, M. and Hegarty, S. (1985). *The Best of Both Worlds . . . ? A Review of Research into the Education of Pupils of South Asian Origin*. London: NFER-Nelson.

Torbe, M. and Medway, P. (1981). *The Climate for Learning*. London: Ward Lock Educational.

Worpole, K. (1977). Beyond the classroom walls. In Hoyles, M. (ed.), *The Politics of Literacy*. London: Writers and Readers Publishing Cooperative.

2 Children's books in a multicultural world: A view from the USA

RUDINE SIMS BISHOP

> Since I don't see myself or most people I know in most things I see or read about Black people, I can't be bothered with that. I wish you could read something or see a movie that would show the people just, well, as my grandmother would say, drylongso. You know, like most of us really are most of the time – together enough to do what we have to do to be decent people.
>
> (Harriet Jones, cited in Gwaltney, 1980)

Readers seek their reflections in books. For people who find themselves marginalized because of race, religion, ethnicity, class, gender or age, the book as mirror reaffirms their existence, and confirms the legitimacy of their attempts to be 'decent people' in their own society. The importance of the book as mirror is demonstrated in an anecdote related in the *Horn Book* by Julius Lester (1984), an African-American writer. When he was living in New York City, Lester frequented a branch of the New York Public Library, and became fascinated by the borrowing habits of a group of elderly women who patronized the same library. He observed that these women seemed to read mystery and detective novels exclusively, borrowing six or seven each week. Lester was intrigued, but after re-reading a few mysteries himself, he understood the attraction they held for those readers. Many of the detectives in those books, like Agatha Christies's Miss Marple, were themselves older women. Lester (1984: 165) concluded that:

> There is no other literary genre in which old women are treated with dignity, respect, and love. The old women, alone in life, forgotten and useless to society, had found their mirrors and thus mitigated what could have been a crushing loneliness into a solitary warmth.

Not all readers are as successful as Lester's old women in discovering their own reflections in books. Those least likely to do so are members of cultural groups, particularly people of colour, which are not dominant in the society of which they are a part. Harriet Jones, the 16-year-old pseudonymous

African-American speaker cited in the epigraph for this chapter, sought her mirror in books and media, and, finding none, refused to 'be bothered with' the available images offered there.

Laurence Yep (1987), a Chinese-American writer, relates what it was like to try to build 'a Chinese sense of reality' as background for writing *Dragonwings*, a novel about Chinese immigrants in turn-of-the-century San Francisco:

> I felt very much like the Invisible Man, without form and without shape. It was as if all the features on my face had been erased and I was just a blank mirror reflecting other people's hopes and fears. And if I wanted to see any features on my face, I would have to go through a Hollywood prop room and go digging around for masks . . . The best thing I could have hoped for would have involved going from Hollywood to literature; then I could be the intelligent dependable sidekick like Lee in *East of Eden*.
>
> (Yep, 1987: 495)

The comments of Yep and 'Jones' delineate the potential power of books – and other media – to affect the way people see themselves as well as the ways they are seen by others. In a society such as the USA where there are not only multiple cultural groups, but where generally those groups that are identifiable by skin colour are victimized by racism, books can serve as important weapons against that racism, for children of both the dominant and non-dominant groups.

The potential benefits of having books about people of colour available for children who are members of those groups are obvious: a sense of belonging, improved self-concept, a transmission of the values of the home culture, a sense of their own history. But, equally important, are the potential benefits of such books for those children who are members of the dominant groups. They have always found their mirrors in children's books, but because they have not found others presented, like Lester's old women, 'with dignity, respect, and love', they have also been given an exaggerated sense of their own importance. Even worse, books which have offered negative stereotypes have perpetuated racism, and fostered a dangerous sense of superiority among white children of dominant groups. To an important degree, those children have been denied the benefits of books as windows onto worlds and people different from, and yet similar to, themselves. They have been denied a full understanding of what it means to be human, of their connections to all other humans in a world populated by a wide variety of peoples and cultures.

Of necessity, this chapter focuses on the situation related to children's books in the multicultural society that is the USA. I recognize that the USA does not represent the world, that the situation there is not the same as the situation in the rest of the English-speaking world, that indeed the situation there is unique. I also recognize, however, that where there are societies with dominant and non-dominant groups, the experience of the non-dominant groups in one country will find echoes in the experiences of similar groups in other countries. I hope, therefore, that teachers in the UK and other English-speaking countries will find this chapter useful and relevant. I begin with a description of the current scene in the USA regarding children's literature about so-called minorities, and a discussion of trends of the 1980s and early 1990s. That description will be followed by an examination of the issues involved in selecting and evaluating such books. Finally, I will focus on pedagogy and some suggestions for incorporating multicultural literature into classroom curricula.

The current scene

Even as we near the end of the twentieth century, teachers who seek to use literature to promote multiculturalism find that task complicated by insufficient books that include or feature people of colour, and by the necessity to select and evaluate such books using criteria in addition to the commonly accepted literary ones. The current scene in multicultural books can be better understood in the context of a piece of recent history.

In the USA, four groups constitute the major racial minorities: African-American, Latinos (Hispanics), Asian-Americans and Native Americans (Indians). The Asian and Latino populations continue to grow rapidly, but components (e.g. Chinese, Japanese, Puerto Ricans) of all the larger groups have had a presence in the country for at least 150 years. Yet the availability of books by and about members of those groups is both limited and skewed. It is difficult to assemble a high-quality collection of books, especially contemporary fiction, about Latinos, Asian-Americans or Native Americans. On the other hand, a relatively large number of books about contemporary Blacks is available, but despite a Black presence in this country that goes back more than 350 years, that has been the case only in the last 25 years or so. In 1965, research showed that the US world of children's books was virtually 'all-white'; only 6.6 per cent of the books published in the USA from 1962 to 1964 included even one Black character in the text or illustrations (Larrick, 1965). Only 0.8 per cent of those books featured contemporary American Blacks. By the mid-1970s, civil rights activism, government programmes and a liberal social climate had combined to increase substantially the numbers of books about African-Americans, and to encourage and support a number of writers from the African-American community. Ten years after Larrick's article, Virginia Hamilton became the first Black author to receive the John Newbery Medal, the most prestigious award for children's literature in the USA.

The social climate and the availability of government funds for libraries also stimulated an increase in the number of books about other groups, but not to the same extent as books about African-Americans. The reasons for this dearth of materials about other peoples of colour remain unclear, but one likely reason is that the market for such books is perceived to be very limited. At the end of the 1980s, African-Americans represented about 12.5 per cent of the population, Latinos about 8 per cent and others about 3 per cent. The major market for books about minorities is still perceived to be the groups themselves, or the schools and libraries which serve them. Since many people of colour in the USA have low incomes, they are not generally thought of as spending a lot of money on books. And since we have not yet arrived at the point where it is considered important for all children to have access to books as windows on their multicultural world, whites in more affluent communities are not yet perceived of as being potential buyers of books about non-dominant minorities.

If the 1960s and 1970s fostered a liberal social environment, the 1980s ushered in an age of conservatism. Government funds for libraries were substantially reduced. The numbers of books about African-Americans decreased accordingly, so that only about 1 per cent (an average of 20 books per year) of all children's books published in the USA between 1980 and 1983 were in that category (Sims, 1985). An even smaller percentage of the books published featured other people of colour; new books featuring other minorities became nearly as scarce as the proverbial 'hen's teeth'.

At present, the situation seems to be changing for the better. Demographic data indicate that the fastest growing groups in the USA are Asians and Hispanics. Within the next decade, many cities will find that the so-called minorities will constitute the majority of the school population. In California at present, no one racial or ethnic group constitutes the majority of the state population. These data, coupled with a general increase in children's book publishing, and the current focus on multicultural curricula, have spurred an increase in the numbers of children's books about people of colour.

One resource that gives some insight into the current scene in the USA is the 1989 edition of *The Black Experience in Children's Books*, an annotated bibliography published every 5 years by the New York Public Library. This bibliography is the most comprehensive listing of children's books about Blacks that is readily available in the USA. The 1989 edition lists approximately 480 books, an increase of about 40 titles on 1984. (The 1984 edition was about half as large as the 1974 edition, demonstrating dramatically the way in which changes in the social climate were reflected in the publishing of children's books.) Of the 480 books listed in the 1989 edition, about 171 were new to the bibliography; that is, they were published between 1984 and 1988. On average, that is 34 titles per year, less than 1.5 per cent of the 2500–3000 children's books published each year in the USA during that period. As the total number of children's books published in the USA has reached 5000 and more per year, there has been a concomitant increase in the number of books about Blacks being published. The percentage, however, has remained about the same. Nevertheless, there is reason for optimism.

Recent trends: What is available?

On both sides of the Atlantic, there is increased attention to the need for multicultural literature to serve multicultural populations. The Cooperative Children's Book Center (Kruse and Horning, 1991) at the University of Wisconsin publishes an annotated bibliography, *Multicultural Children's and Young Adult Literature*, which lists more than 475 selected books published in the USA and Canada from 1980 to 1990. Three guides from Britain indicate that the pluralism that is so much a part of the US life is also a major aspect of modern British society. The *ATCAL Reading Guides* (Stephens, 1988), compiled by the Association for the Teaching of Caribbean, African, Asian and Associated Literatures, provides information about African, Caribbean and Indo-British literature for secondary schools. *Books for Keeps* has published two guides (Triggs, 1985, 1986) which examine books suitable for children aged 12 years and under. At the back of the guides are listings of organizations, journals and other resources useful for teachers with an interest in multicultural literature. The rationale for the *Books for Keeps* guides reminds its readers that British society is 'multi-cultural, multi-ethnic, multi-lingual, multi-faith', (p. 1). In the past 20 years, that pluralism has begun to be reflected in some of the literature that has been made available to British children.

As attention to multicultural literature has increased, so has the range of types and topics of available books. Generally, books with multicultural themes and topics are of four types. In the discussion that follows, I have, where possible, used as examples books available both in the USA and Britain.

The first type of book is consciously inter-racial. Such books are either visually integrated, simply including pictures of various and diverse children participating in whatever activity is being depicted, or they focus on people of different backgrounds interacting with each other. In either case, they project a vision of a multicultural, multiracial society. One place increased visual integration is evident is in some of the newer books for babies and young children such as the Ahlbergs' *The Baby's Catalogue*, Helen Oxenbury's *All Fall Down* and Tony Bradman's *The Bad Babies' Counting Book*. Concept books and non-fiction for younger and older children are also much more likely to include illustrations of children from diverse backgrounds than was the case a few years ago. In the USA at least, many such books are illustrated with photographs, such as George Ancona's *Helping Out* or Jill Krementz's *How It Feels When Parents Divorce*. Examples of books which focus on interactions among people of different racial or cultural backgrounds are Tony Bradman's *Through My Window* and Shirley

Hughes' *Alfie Gives a Hand*. One of the 1991 Caldecott Honor Books, Vera Williams' *'More, More, More!' Said the Baby*, features babies and loving parents from different racial groups, including a Black child with a blonde Caucasian grandmother.

A second group of books projects a sense that people are people are people. These books feature children of colour, but there is no attempt to reflect a culture distinct from the shared dominant one. The child could be a member of any cultural group within the larger society. One such book, *Ten, Nine, Eight* by Molly Bang, features a Black child and her father at bedtime. Another is Ann Jonas's *Holes and Peeks*, in which a Black child is frightened by large holes, but amused by small ones through which she can peek. An interesting confirmation of the 'people are people' quality of those two books is that, in the US publication *Multicultural Children's and Young Adult Literature* (Kruse and Horning, 1991), the girls in both books are described as 'African-American', whereas in the *Books for Keeps* guide, no mention is made of the US origin of the books and the girls are described merely as 'Black'. Whether they are American or British does not matter. Done well, this kind of book has the merit of depicting its characters positively as participants in the 'mainstream', reflecting the experiences of many so-called minority families, and aspects of the experience of others.

A third set of books focuses directly on the distinctive experience of being a 'drylongso' human being within a particular cultural group. While there may be characters from other groups, integration is not the focus. The extent to which a distinct culture is reflected may vary from the very subtle incorporation of values and attitudes in an otherwise 'people are people' story, to a reflection of distinctive language patterns, to a conscious effort on the part of the author to portray some particular aspect of the specific culture. Obadiah's *I Am a Rastafarian* in the *Books for Keeps* guides is a good example featuring a British family. From the USA, the fictional works of Virginia Hamilton (e.g. *M.C. Higgins, the Great*; *Sweet Whispers, Brother Rush*) and Rosa Guy (e.g. *The Friends*; *Paris, Pee Wee, and Big Dog*) exemplify this type of book. It should be pointed out that the experience of any one group is not monolithic. Reflecting 'the Black experience' in the USA, for example, does not mean that a book must be set in the inner city and feature characters who are economically poor.

A fourth type focuses specifically on coping with racism and discrimination. The most powerful such books set in the USA are the novels and novellas of Mildred Taylor: *Roll of Thunder, Hear My Cry*; *Let the Circle Be Unbroken*; *The Road to Memphis*; *The Gold Cadillac*; *The Friendship*; *Mississippi Bridge*. Other such books, set in South Africa, are Beverley Naidoo's *Journey to Jo'Burg: A South African Story* and its sequel *Chain of Fire*.

In general in the USA in the past few years, there has been an increase in the number of books that include diverse children in all kinds of settings.

These are one of the few sources of books as mirrors for children of colour other than African-Americans. The 'people are people' books featuring Black children continue to be published at a relatively steady rate, as do those reflecting distinctive African-American experiences and culture. Compared to the late 1960s, very few 'problem books' focusing on racism and discrimination are being published in the USA today.

Regarding genre, *The Black Experience* bibliography is instructive about the situation in the USA. Of the 171 new books listed, 57 (one-third) are biographies. It is especially noteworthy that the list of biographies is no longer dominated by sports and entertainment figures, but includes people who have been active politically or who have made contributions to the arts and sciences. Also noteworthy is the increase in the number of books about, or set in, the Caribbean and Africa. Forty-nine of the 171 new books fall into those categories, including a number of biographies of prominent Africans, most notably Archbishop Tutu and Winnie Mandela.

The *Black Experience* bibliography does not include books published since 1988. My own library, however, leaves me optimistic about the most recent picture books featuring African-Americans. To the extent that my relatively small sample can be said to indicate trends, I have identified the following: (1) increasing attention to African-American, as opposed to African, folklore; (2) a new focus on nostalgic family stories in which parents share stories about their own growing up, or in which adults reminisce about their childhood; (3) the use of the paintings of well-known artists such as Romare Bearden as illustrations; (4) an increase in fantasy; (5) increased attention to Caribbean backgrounds and settings; (6) some attention to books for the very young featuring Black children exclusively. My sense is that these 'microtrends' signal a widening of the range and scope of picture books about Blacks.

The one genre that is consistently able to offer some reflections of root cultures is folklore. In the USA, numerous folk tales continue to be available in picture book format. African and Native American tales have been joined recently by tales from the Caribbean, from Central and South America and the Asian countries from which immigrants, old and new, have come (e.g. China, Japan, Vietnam, Korea).

Some of the recent activity can be attributed to two factors – the continued presence of a group of Black authors and illustrators in the USA and UK, and the emergence of small presses. In the USA, Black writers whose work began appearing in the late 1960s and early 1970s (e.g. Virginia Hamilton, Eloise Greenfield, Lucille Clifton, Walter Dean Myers, Rosa Guy and Mildred Taylor) have been joined by others, such as illustrators Pat Cummings and Jerry Pinkney, and writer/storyteller Patricia McKissack. Unfortunately, it is difficult to name more than one or two prominent writers or illustrators who are Native American, Latino or Asian-American. In the UK, well-known writers and artists like Buchi Emecheta, Petronella

Breinberg, James Berry, John Agard, Errol Lloyd and Farrukh Dhondy reflect the African, Caribbean and Indian peoples who are part of that society.

In recent years, some of the book production reflecting the cultural experiences of people of colour in the USA and UK has been among the small, 'alternative' presses. Rosemary Stones (1986), writing in one of the *Books for Keeps* guides, indicates that the small presses in Britain have developed in response to dissatisfaction with mainstream publishing, and in an effort to offer the kind of multicultural books which were needed but not forthcoming. In the USA, one of the most visible of the small presses is Children's Book Press, which publishes books in Spanish and English relating to Latin America and the Caribbean, as well as 'Asian-America, Africa and Native America'. They claim in their catalogue to be 'the only children's publisher offering contemporary legends based on tales from the minority and refugee communities . . . in North America'. Clearly, the small presses are serving the important function of increasing the quality and quantity of multicultural books.

Issues in selecting and evaluating books for multicultural classrooms

Increased numbers of books with a multicultural theme or about people of colour mean increased responsibility for carefully and thoughtfully selecting the books to be used in classrooms. Books have always reflected the society of which they are a part, and the history of race relations in the USA and UK has not been particularly constructive. This history has been reflected in children's books in two ways in particular: too few books which include people of colour and, when they have been published, the negative stereotypes and other visual and verbal images and messages they contain have helped to shape the racial attitudes of generations. This means that today's teachers, librarians, writers, editors and publishers, whatever their ethnicity or racial background, have been partly socialized by a literature that has, at minimum, not been designed to promote a multicultural world, and at worst has perpetuated racist notions of how the world is and should be. This is not to imply any deliberate racist behaviour on their part, but only to assert the need for a conscious effort to overcome the effects of past social history.

Whatever their attitudes about past history and its effect on themselves, teachers, librarians and parents believe that books and stories have the power to help socialize children by transmitting our values, our biases and our perspectives on the world. This belief in the perceived power of the written word is the spur to many of the censorship debates that rage over books which one group or another sees as alien to their beliefs, repugnant to their sense of morality or damaging to their self-concepts.

Nevertheless, purists assert that the only criteria by which literature needs to be evaluated are such time-honoured literary ones as these: Is the plot original and plausible? Is the theme worthy and skilfully woven into the book? Are the characterizations strong? Is the author's style noteworthy? Those criteria should be, of course, the first to be applied, since no classroom or library should be stocked with books of inferior quality, and the inclusion of people of colour or multiracial or multicultural themes is no reason to follow a different policy. Long ago, Walter de la Mare asserted that only the rarest kind of best is good enough for children, and if that assertion is true at all, it is no less applicable to children of colour.

Literary criteria, however, are not the only ones to be applied to books which include people of colour. If such books are to provide mirrors for some children and windows for others, the images they offer ought to be clear and undistorted. Broderick (1973), Brown (1933) and others have documented the historical treatment of African-Americans in children's and adult literature of the nineteenth century as well as the first half of the twentieth century. Nor have African-Americans been the only peoples subjected to such ridicule or negative stereotypes in children's books. In the USA, Native Americans, Latinos and Asians have all been portrayed in stereotypical ways (see, e.g. Stensland, 1979; Nieto, 1983; Slapin and Seale, 1988). The readiest examples come from the more abundant books which include, or are about, African-Americans. To the extent that the experience of one undervalued minority group is echoed in the experiences of others, books about African-Americans will serve, in the following discussion, as representative. The specifics will be different for other groups, but the principles seem to apply. Gillian Klein's book, *Reading Into Racism* (1985), for example, examines the issues as they are manifest in Britain, and provides many similar examples.

Fortunately, the blatant minstrel images and plantation stereotypes, the watermelon-eating, grinning, bug-eyed 'darkies' have all but disappeared from US children's literature. *Little Black Sambo*, however, is still with us in its 'authorized American version' (Bannerman, n.d.), and unfortunately teachers are still asking 'what's wrong with *Little Black Sambo*? It's such a cute little story.' What is wrong, of course, is that the 'cute little story', supposedly set in India, perpetuates a distorted, caricatured visual image of Blacks as minstrels, ridicules African languages (mumbo-jumbo) and offers a handy epithet (Sambo) that was pejorative even at the end of the nineteenth century when the book was first published. The point is not to launch here yet another attack on *Sambo*, but to reaffirm how strong is the need even now for awareness and sensitivity on the part of those who select books and read them to children.

If today's writers and artists are no longer creating Little Black Sambos, we are not yet totally free of negative stereotyping in children's books. Readers familiar with the first edition of the still best-selling *Charlie and the Chocolate Factory* by Roald Dahl will remember the not-quite-human oompa-loompas and the flap that caused them to be made into somewhat less clear caricatures of Africans in later editions. As late as 1984, a less well-known retelling of an African-American folk tale was the target of the following remarks in a *Horn Book* review: 'an unbelievable combination of stereotyping, violence, and blasphemy. The black-and-white illustrations are unfunny, crude, ugly, and offensive' (Howard, 1984).

Because one of the most easily observable markers of cultural group membership – as well as social class status – is language, an author's use of dialect can also become an issue in evaluating children's books. Dialect can be used to ridicule, making characters appear stupid and incapable of learning the language around them, especially if that happens to be the prestige dialect, the standard language of the country. Such use of dialect was common in series of books popular for some time in the USA, such as *The Bobbsey Twins*, which featured Black servants whose language was a caricature of low-status Black speech. More modern books, however, tend to reflect more accurately the everyday speech of the characters they portray. Dialect is used, not for comedy, but as part of the delineation of the characters. It is often used very effectively by authors whose ear for the language they recreate is finely tuned. Eloise Greenfield's work, for example, often reflects aspects of informal Black vernacular. Walter Dean Myers, who writes about Black teenagers in urban settings, is especially adept at representing the typical language of Black boys growing up in US cities.

In the USA, when dialect becomes an issue, it is often because parents and teachers object to any presentation of non-standard English to their children because they understand the low esteem in which that language is held, and they expect the school to enable their children to be speakers of standard English. It also becomes an issue when teachers feel that they cannot effectively read aloud a story or poem that is written in a dialect different from their own, or that their attempts will be found offensive by their pupils or their parents.

A second linguistic issue concerns the use of foreign languages, and their dialects. Nieto (1983) explains the kinds of errors made by authors who incorporate Spanish phrases and names into books about US Latinos: misspellings, inaccurate idioms, borrowings from Italian, borrowings from one Spanish-speaking group in stories about another (e.g. the use of Mexican phrases in stories about Puerto Ricans). In a multilingual society, the use of languages other than English, handled with care, has the potential to enrich the literature, and help develop in readers' understandings about the linguistic diversity that is an important part of a multicultural world.

Generally, however, the concerns of today centre on subtle issues, often related to how people of colour are valued in the books in which they are portrayed. This valuation is often directly related to the perspective from which the author views his or her characters. The author's perspective affects, and is affected by, a number of factors: the sense of audience, the sense of purpose, the choice of which details to use to delineate setting and develop character, the accuracy with which those details are described.

In the following discussion, the designation 'primary audience' is not intended to imply that any book is consciously meant to be closed to any group of readers, but to relate that my reading of books about Blacks and others suggests that some authors seem primarily to write *about* Blacks, whereas others seem consciously to write *to*, or even *for*, them, and the resulting books differ in predictable ways. The author's perceived primary audience can help to determine whether people of colour are presented as comic relief, as savages in need to conquering or civilizing, as persons in need of paternalistic aid, or as fully functioning, well-rounded human beings. It is unlikely that Helen Bannerman saw her primary reading audience as little Black children; nor, for that matter, did Edgar Allen Poe see Blacks as the audience for *The Gold Bug*. Thus their Black characters seem merely for the amusement of their white readers. Numerous examples could be cited from nineteenth- and early twentieth-century history, but the issue remains in more recent books, though more subtly. During the late 1960s and early 1970s, a spate of books appeared in the USA which focused on desegregating schools and neighbourhoods. In almost all of those books, the apparent primary audience was white children, and the primary theme (or in some cases, moral) had to do with how they ought to behave in the face of changes in the racial make-up of 'their' schools and communities. Often, the relationship between the white and Black characters was clearly paternalistic.

When authors and artists assume their audience to be multiracial and multicultural, often the result is a book which consciously depicts multiracial and multicultural children, or a 'people are people' book in which the characters may be Black, Asian or Latino, but their experiences are 'universal' (sometimes interpreted to mean 'common to white Western society, or even the USA'). In some cases, the characters could, on some level, be interchangeable; that is, if an Asian child were replaced in a later edition by a white one, for instance, it would not matter except that there would be one less book in which an Asian child could find her mirror; the book itself could remain otherwise unchanged.

Authors who perceive their primary audience as being members of so-called minority groups usually have a character from that group as the protagonist, and often – though not always – depict the distinctiveness of the experience of growing up as a member of a particular cultural group. Some authors are more successful than others, depending on their knowledge of the culture and the details of what makes it distinct. Black authors writing about Blacks, for instance, often include references to Black music, religion, history, food and cultural heroes as part of their novels.

Perspective is also affected by a sense of purpose. Fortunately, good modern books are not primarily didactic, and I am not here referring to moral lessons to be learned from books. Good books, however, do have discernible themes, and those, too, sometimes differ with the author's presumed purpose. For example, the white author of *A Girl Called Boy*, a story about a modern African-American girl who is transported back to nineteenth-century slavery, saw in slave narratives a 'strength and spirit of sharing' similar to those of her own pioneering ancestors. Therefore, her purpose in writing her novel was to 'capture that same spirit in a story about slave children' (Hurmence, 1982). As I have asserted elsewhere (Sims, 1984), Hurmence appears ultimately to want to help socialize her readers into the larger American society, helping them to focus on those attributes shared across the various cultural groups that make up the larger American society.

Many American Black authors, on the other hand, seem intent on socializing their Black readers by helping them understand what it means to grow up Black in the USA; to transmit their sense of what kind of behaviours, attitudes and knowledge are valued in the Black community. Thus, certain themes seem to be common to the works of many Black writers. The major overarching theme of fiction by Black writers in the USA is survival – the will and strength that have enabled the group to survive both physically and psychologically. Related sub-themes involve a strong sense of community; the importance of human relationships, especially within the family; pride in one's blackness; and the importance of one's history and heritage.

An author's perspective is also sometimes relevant in his or her selection of detail (e.g. images, events, activities) and the accuracy with which those details are rendered. The white author who chose to describe her Black protagonist as 'different and comical looking *oozing like dark dough over her last-year's Sunday dress*' (emphasis added), and her father's hands like 'spiders about to jump' (Sebestyn, 1979), betrayed a perspective on her characters and a standard of beauty unlikely to have been shaped in a Black community. On the other hand, Virginia Hamilton (1971: 37) employs a different standard when she describes her character Zeely as 'six and a half feet tall, thin and deeply dark as a pole of Ceylon ebony . . . her thin oblong head didn't seem to fit quite right on her shoulders . . . the face was the most beautiful she had ever seen'. In contrast to the spider-like hands of Sebestyn's Black father, Hamilton's character's 'fingers looked exactly like bean pods left a long time in the sun'. The aforementioned historical novel by Hurmence (*A Girl Called Boy*) is full of details that betray her perspective on the slave experience of the American South as relatively more benign than it is generally seen by Black Americans.

An author's perspective also affects the ways in which characters are presented and developed. As portrayed by some white authors, for example (Theodore Taylor in *The Cay*, Ouida Sebestyn in *Words By Heart*), exemplary Black men are often servile and self-sacrificing. Mildred Taylor's exemplary Black hero, David Logan, in contrast, refuses to be subservient, though he carefully considers when and how and for what causes he is willing to take a stand and to risk his life.

The issue of perspective – when evaluating books about people of colour – is often over-simplified to the question of whether whites can or should write about people of colour. The issue is, however, much more subtle and complicated than that. Unfortunately, writers who are members of non-dominant groups are not immune from having absorbed some of the negative attitudes held about their own group by others. In those cases, their negative attitudes towards their own group will be reflected in their work. Some white writers, from their own vantage point, can create works about Blacks that are positive and noteworthy. The race of the author is not the point; the perspective of the author is what matters and what determines, in some cases, whether the book is successful at all, and, in others, in what ways and how effectively it succeeds in fulfilling the author's purpose or in satisfying its readers' needs.

Multicultural literature in the classroom

Issues and controversies notwithstanding, teachers who wish to incorporate multicultural literature into their syllabuses will find a fair number of high-quality books available. Teachers will find their own ways to use such books, but the following may offer some food for thought, some support for work already being done, or perhaps even some new ideas.

The major task for teachers who wish to use literary materials for developing multicultural understandings is to make that goal an integral part of the planning and conducting of classroom experiences and activities. In the USA, February is Black History Month. It is the one time in the year when some Black authors, illustrators and community leaders can be assured of abundant invitations to visit schools. It is also the time when students will be required to read biographies, informational books, poetry and novels by and about Blacks. One can only assume that during the remainder of the year, in schools where there are no or few Black students, no effort is made to continue the same kinds of activities. Those kinds of once-a-year experiences, or even the special 'units' focusing on particular groups (e.g. in the USA, a typical theme might be 'Indians'), run the risk of keeping the group on the margins of society, and focusing children's attention on the 'differentness' and the 'quaint customs' of the groups (teepees, pow-wows and rain dances). The alternative is to be certain that, whatever the area of study, if it is supported by literature, the books offered to students represent a variety of the people and cultures present in a heterogeneous society.

Folklore, for example, is a rich source for developing multicultural awareness and understandings about the similarities and differences among humans. When tales from various cultural groups are available in class-rooms, there are opportunities to make connections, and to celebrate those similarities and differences. Commonly known European tales such as those collected by the Brothers Grimm can be joined on classroom shelves by collections from many other cultures. One example is Virginia Hamilton's *The People Could Fly*, a collection of Black American folk tales. The author's notes may help to provide context and background information where needed. Stories from Africa, India and the Caribbean are also readily available. Where printed tales are difficult to find, it is possible to tap the classroom and the community it serves for stories. All groups have stories, and children, their parents, their grandparents and others in the community can be invited to share theirs in the classroom. Literature need not come in the form of a book.

Picture books and printed collections of folk tales abound, however, and they offer numerous opportunities for focusing on multiculturalism. Students can be helped to discover, for example, that variants of the same tales, motifs and types of tales appear across world cultures. The usual European versions of 'Cinderella' ('Tattercoats', 'The Glass Slipper') can be examined alongside other versions, e.g. the Chinese *Yeh Shen* by Ai Ling Louie, *The Egyptian Cinderella* by Ruth Heller or John Steptoe's *Mufaro's Beautiful Daughters*, a South African tale. After such stories have been enjoyed for their own sake, students can be led to compare them with a view to understanding in what ways they are variations of the same tale (or include some motifs in common), and how the differences in detail may in some way reflect the cultures and geography of the places and peoples from which the stories came.

A look at certain motifs can also illuminate the similarities among peoples of various groups. The 'trickster' character, for example, is present in many cultures. In West Africa, the USA and the Caribbean, for example, Ananse (Anansi, Aunt Nancy, etc.) is the spider/human trickster who is central to numerous tales. He is the one who won all the world's stories from the sky god Nyame in Gail Haley's *A Story, A Story*, and the one who is outsmarted in Verna Aardema's *Oh, Kojo! How Could You?* Other tricksters include the fox in Russia and the coyote among some Native American tribes of the Pacific Northwest in the USA and Canada.

A study of types of tales can also develop understandings about how story has functioned for human beings all over the world. Porquoi tales demonstrate human attempts to explain animal characteristics or human customs. *Why Mosquitos Buzz in People's Ears* is an example by Aardema from West Africa. The origin of purring is explained in a Caribbean tale, *The Cat's Purr*, retold and illustrated by Ashley Bryan. 'Why the Bear is Stumpy-tailed' comes from Norway.

Story has also functioned as a means to explore questions about the origin and meaning of life, of humans' relationships to and with natural and super-natural forces and beings. Those stories have formed mythologies, and the introduction of myths from cultures in addition to the classical Greek and Roman ones can enrich a classroom. Virginia Hamilton recently published *In the Beginning*, a collection of creation myths which beautifully demonstrates how people from around the world have tried to answer the singular question, 'How did the world and its people come to be?'

Poetry also offers ample opportunities for helping students make connections. Collections of Mother Goose rhymes that are illustrated with children of various hues and set in modern times re-interpret the rhymes in a way that invites all children to make them their own. Similarly, introducing collections of children's playground rhymes and other street rhymes and jingles is a way to include everyone. In the USA, for example, Cheryl Warren Mattox has published *Shake It To the One That You Love the Best*, a collection of African-American playsongs and lullabies. The *Books for Keeps* guide for children aged 7 years and under describes a collection compiled by P. Edwards, called *Inky Pinky Ponky: Children's Playground Rhymes*. Where such collections are not readily available, children can be guided to create their own.

Teachers can also look for and introduce poets and poetry from diverse cultures. For example, in *Say It Again, Granny*, the Guyanese poet John Agard has presented 20 poems based on Caribbean proverbs. Aside from enjoying the language and wisdom of the poems and proverbs, students will be reminded of the sayings of their own grandmothers, and can be encouraged to compare, to find how different groups have different ways of expressing similar aphoristic meanings. Other anthologies or individual poems by poets from various cultures can enrich classrooms by supplying a multiplicity of voices, rhythms and imagery, and emotions.

Both folk tales and poetry also provide opportunities to examine, consider and develop respect for dialect differences. When numerous dialects are a natural part of the classroom, it becomes easier to understand that variation and change are natural aspects of living languages. Further, considerations of how the same meaning may be expressed in different dialects can demonstrate the aptness of the author's use of language that befits a character and his or her time and place. Teachers and others who read aloud such works will need to practise in order to offer their readings with a sense of some accuracy and respect for the language.

To a degree, respect can be developed, and prejudice mitigated by facts. Non-fiction books can offer vital information about the current and past lives of the diverse peoples who comprise a multicultural and multiracial society. In the USA, such books as Milton Meltzer's *The Chinese Americans*, *The Hispanic Americans* and *The Black Americans: In Their Own Words* provide accurate data about the history and contributions of some of the groups which make up American society. Such books can be sources of pride for children from the group portrayed, and educational – in the best sense of the word – for others. They can be a part of a study of the people of a country or a part of broader themes, such as the human effects of world economics (e.g. why do people emigrate from one country to another?).

Many teachers in the USA and Canada are finding value in having small groups of children read and discuss related sets of books with similar themes, artistic styles, genres, structures, etc. Such sets can include, as a matter of course, books featuring characters from diverse groups. For example, a set for young children, focused on 'grandparents', might include the following: Eloise Greenfield's *Grandpa's Face*, which features a Black girl and her actor grandfather; Karen Ackerman's *Song and Dance Man*, in which a white American grandfather entertains his grandchildren with his old vaudeville act; Eve Bunting's *The Wednesday Surprise*, which shows a young girl helping her European immigrant grandmother learn to read; and Niki Daly's *Not So Fast, Songololo*, which features a young Black boy helping his grandmother on a shopping trip into the city of Johannesburg. A second set might centre on families working together and could include the three Vera Williams picture books (*A Chair for My Mother; Music, Music for Everyone*; and *Something Special for Me*), in which a family without much money saves together for necessities and gifts, and Valerie Flournoy's *The Patchwork Quilt* in which a Black family works together to complete a quilt begun by Tanya's grandmother. Comparisons can reinforce the sense of human similarity, while at the same time celebrate our uniquenesses.

Some teachers also find success in devoting a few weeks to exploring a theme, such as 'Newcomers' or 'Travellers', and offering students choices of various books and activities related to that theme. Jill Paton Walsh's *The Green Book*, which chronicles the settling of a new planet, Beverley Naidoo's *Journey to Jo'burg*, in which two South African Black children make a long, eye-opening trip to their mother's place of work, Barbara Smucker's *Underground to Canada*, which traces the journey of fugitive slaves from the American South to Canada along the underground railroad, and Nadia Wheatley and Donna Rawlins's *My Place*, an Australian book which chronicles the history of a settlement and the people who lived there from the time of the Aborigines to the present, are examples of books which can fit the theme. In addition to the understandings that might develop from the individual books, the set can be the basis for discussions of questions such as why people might risk travelling to new places, or what kinds of preparations need to be taken for long journeys, or the kinds of receptions strangers receive in new places and why.

The point of all these examples has been to assert that, if literature is to be used to widen students' perspectives, as well as to strengthen their understandings of differences and similarities among human beings, then literature which offers various perspectives and understandings, and which mirrors the experiences of diverse groups of people, must be an integral part of students' everyday school experience.

At the same time as books can be mirrors for some students, they can be windows, or sliding glass doors, through which students can view and participate in the lives of people whose culture and life experiences are different from their own. For example, well-written books open the way to understanding the effects of racist behaviour on both its perpetrators and its victims. This chapter concludes with a discussion of students' response to Mildred Taylor's *The Gold Cadillac*. This discussion is based on the work of Debra Arrowsmith, a graduate student in my class in children's literature. The class had been assigned the task of sharing a book or poem with a group of students and recording and analysing their responses.

The Gold Cadillac tells of an African-American man who, in the early 1950s, buys a new luxury car. Because they had agreed to save for a house, his wife is upset that he hadn't consulted her, and refuses to ride in the car. Their two daughters, however, are excited and pleased with the new car and the status it provides in the community and among the family. The father announces, after a time of showing off the car, that he plans to drive the Cadillac from their home in northern Ohio to visit their family in Mississippi. He persists in his plan despite warnings from his family and friends that a Black man driving through the South in a Cadillac with a northern licence plate is asking for trouble. His wife, seeing how determined he is, announces that she and the girls will accompany him. The trip becomes the girls' introduction to institutional racism – the 'Whites Only' signs on water fountains and restaurants, and the realization that the food and beverages they packed were not a picnic for fun but necessitated by the racial discrimination routinely practised at the time. As they reach Mississippi, they are stopped by white policemen who call the father 'boy', insist that the car must be stolen, arrest him and detain him for 3 hours while the girls and their mother wait in the car. Eventually, they reach their destination and return home safely.

The five children who heard this story were a mixed-race group of eighth graders (12- and 13-year-olds) – one Chinese-American, two African-Americans and two white Americans. During the first half of the story, they were focused on the conflict within the family. One white girl found an echo of her family experience, since her father had once bought a motorcycle without consulting her mother. Others speculated on whether such a thing was likely to happen in their family, and on their opinions of the mother's behaviour: 'My mom would not have made my dad feel so bad about the car. I don't think that's very family-like'; 'My mom . . . would have been just as stubborn'. Having made connections with the book family, and having become involved in their problems, the students reacted with outrage to the family's experiences with racism. The white boy raised a question which demonstrated his growing awareness of its effects: 'If the police did things like that to the Black people, who did they have to go to for protection when most people probably went to a policemen?' His question permitted the Black boy to explain why, historically, accommodation to white racist behaviour was sometimes necessary for the survival of individual Blacks. The white girl summarized the sense of the group: '. . . I even know some people who still say ugly things about individuals all because of the colour of their skin, or because they look and/or talk differently. These people haven't even given the other person a chance!'

For these students, *The Gold Cadillac* was a window onto a world they had not experienced. For some of them, it seemed ancient history; for others, it was closer to home. In any case, their response demonstrates the potential of reading and discussing literature as a way to help students see the connections between themselves and all other human beings; to read, as the title of this volume suggests, against racism, and to think about what it means to be a drylongso, decent human being in their world.

References

Broderick, D. (1973). *Image of the Black in Children's Fiction.* New York: R.R. Bowker.

Brown, S. (1933). Negro classics as seen by white authors. *Journal of Negro education*, 2: 179–203.

Gwaltney, J.H. (1980). *Drylongso.* New York: Random House.

Howard, E.F. (1984). Review of *Big Sixteen* by Mary Calhoun. *Horn Book*, 60: 41–2.

Klein, G. (1985). *Reading into Racism: Bias in Children's Literature and Learning Materials.* London: Routledge and Kegan Paul.

Kruse, G.M. and Horning, K.T. (1991). *Multicultural Children's and Young Adult Literature: A Selected Listing of Books 1980–90 by and about People of Color*, 3rd edn. Madison, Wisconsin: Cooperative Children's Book Center, University of Wisconsin.

Larrick, N. (1965). The all-white world of children's books. *Saturday Review*, 11, September: 63–5, 84–5.

Lester, J. (1984). The beechwood staff. *Horn Book*, 60: 161–9.

New York Public Library Black Experience in Children's Books Committee (1989). *The Black Experience in Children's Books.* New York: New York Public Library.

Nieto, S. (1983). Children's literature on Puerto Rican themes, Parts I and II. *Interracial Books for Children Bulletin*, 14(1,2): 6–16.

Sims, R. (1984). A question of perspective. *The Advocate*, 3, Spring: 145–56.

Sims, R. (1985). Children's books about Blacks: A mid-eighties status report. In Senick, G.J. (ed.), *Children's Literature Review.* Detroit, Mich.: Gale Research.

Slapin, B. and Seale, D. (1988). *Books Without Bias: Through Indian Eyes.* Berkeley, Calif.: Oyate.

Stensland, A. (1979). *Literature by and about the American Indian*, 2nd edn. Urbana, Ill.: National Council of Teachers of English.

Stephens, J. (ed.) (1988). *ATCAL Reading Guides: African, Caribbean, and Indo-British Literature for the Classroom.* London: ATCAL Publications/ ILEA English Centre.

Stones, R. (1986). Voices being heard. In Triggs, P. (ed.), *The Books for Keeps Guide to Children's Books for a Multi-cultural Society, 0–7.* London: Books for Keeps.

Triggs, P. (ed.) (1985). *The Books for Keeps Guide to Children's Books for a Multi-cultural Society, 8–12.* London: Books for Keeps.

Triggs, P. (1986). *The Books for Keeps Guide to Children's Books for a Multi-cultural Society, 0–7*. London: Books for Keeps.

Yep, L. (1987). A Chinese sense of reality. In Harrison, B. and Maguire, G. (eds), *Innocence and Experience: Essays and Conversations on Children's Literature*. New York: Lothrop.

Children's books cited

Aardema, V. (1975). *Why Mosquitos Buzz in People's Ears* (illustrated by L. Dillon and D. Dillon). New York: Dial.

Aardema, V. (1984). *Oh, Kojo! How Could You?* (illustrated by M. Brown). New York: Dial/London: Hamish Hamilton.

Ackerman, K. (1983). *Song and Dance Man* (illustrated by S. Gammel). New York: Knopf.

Agard, J. (1986). *Say It Again, Granny* (illustrated by S. Gretz). London: Bodley Head.

Ahlberg, J. and Ahlberg, A. (1983). *The Baby's Catalogue*. London: Viking/Boston: Atlantic Monthly Press and Little Brown.

Ancona, G. (1985). *Helping Out*. New York: Clarion.

Bang, M. (1983). *Ten, Nine, Eight*. New York: Greenwillow/London: Julia Macrae.

Bannerman, H. (n.d.). *Little Black Sambo* (authorized American version). New York: J.B. Lippincott.

Bradman, T. (1986). *The Bad Babies' Counting Book* (illustrated by D. van der Beek). London: Picadilly Press/New York: Atheneum.

Bradman, T. (1987). *Through My Window* (illustrated by E. Browne). London: Methuen/Boston: Silver Burdette.

Bryan, A. (1985). *The Cat's Purr*. New York: Atheneum.

Bunting, E. (1989). *The Wednesday Surprise* (illustrated by D. Carrick). New York: Clarion.

Dahl, R. (1964). *Charlie and the Chocolate Factory*. New York: Knopf.

Daly, N. (1985). *Not So Fast, Songololo*. New York: Atheneum/London: Gollancz.

Edwards, P. (1987). *Inky, Pinky, Ponky*. London: Longman.

Flournoy, V. (1985). *The Patchwork Quilt* (illustrated by J. Pinkney). New York: Dial/London: Bodley Head.

Greenfield, E. (1988). *Grandpa's Face* (illustrated by F. Cooper). New York: Philomel.

Guy, R. (1973). *The Friends*. New York: Holt/London: Puffin.

Guy, R. (1984). *Paris, Peewee, and Big Dog*. New York: Delacorte/London: Gollancz and Puffin.

Haley, G. (1970). *A Story, A Story*. New York: Atheneum/London: Methuen.

Hamilton, V. (1974). *M.C. Higgins, The Great*. New York: Macmillan/London: Hamish Hamilton.

Hamilton, V. (1982). *Sweet Whispers, Brother Rush*. New York: Philomel.

Hamilton, V. (1985). *The People Could Fly: Black American Folk Tales* (illustrated by L. Dillon and D. Dillon). New York: Knopf/London: Walker Books.

Hamilton, V. (1988). *In the Beginning: Creation Stories From Around the World* (illustrated by B. Moser). San Diego, Calif.: Harcourt Brace Jovanovich.

Heller, R. (1989). *The Egyptian Cinderella*. New York: Crowell.

Hughes, S. (1984). *Alfie Gives a Hand*. London: Bodley Head/New York: Lothrop.

Hurmence, B. (1982). *A Girl Called Boy*. New York: Clarion.

Jonas, A. (1984). *Holes and Peeks*. New York: Greenwillow/London: Julia MacRae.

Krementz, J. (1984). *How It Feels When Parents Divorce*. New York: Knopf.

Louie, A.L. (1982). *Yeh Shen: A Cinderella Story from China* (illustrated by E. Young). New York: Philomel.

Mattox, C.W. (1989). *Shake It to the One That You Love Best: Playsongs and Lullabies from Black Musical Traditions*. (illustrated by V.P. Honeywood and B. Joysmith). El Sobrante, Calif.: Warren-Mattox Productions.

Meltzer, M. (1980). *The Chinese Americans*. New York: Crowell.

Meltzer, M. (1982). *The Hispanic Americans*. New York: Crowell.

Meltzer, M. (1984). *The Black Americans: In Their Own Words*. New York: Crowell.

Naidoo, B. (1986). *Journey to Jo'burg: A South African Story*. London: Longman/ New York: J.B. Lippincott.

Naidoo, B. (1990). *Chain of Fire*. New York: J.B. Lippincott.

Obadiah (1987). *I am a Rastafarian*. London: Franklin Watts.

Oxenbury, H. (1987). *All Fall Down*. London: Walker Books.

Sebestyn, Q. (1979). *Words by Heart*. New York: Little, Brown.

Smucker, B. (1977). *Underground to Canada*. Toronto: Clarke, Irwin (published under the title *Runaway to Freedom* by Harper in the USA).

Steptoe, J. (1987). *Mufaro's Beautiful Daughters*. New York: Lothrop.

Taylor, M. (1976). *Roll of Thunder, Hear My Cry*. New York: Dial/London: Puffin Plus.

Taylor, M. (1981). *Let the Circle Be Unbroken*. New York: Dial/London: Puffin Plus.

Taylor, M. (1987). *The Friendship*. New York: Dial.

Taylor, M. (1987). *The Gold Cadillac*. New York: Dial.

Taylor, M. (1990). *Mississippi Bridge*. New York: Dial.

Taylor, M. (1990). *The Road to Memphis*. New York: Dial.

Taylor, T. (1969). *The Cay*. New York: Doubleday.

Walsh, J.P. (1982). *The Green Book*. New York: Farrar, Straus and Giroux.

Wheatley, N. and Rawlins, D. (1987). *My Place*. Blackburn, Victoria: Collins Dove.

Williams, V. (1982). *A Chair for My Mother*. New York: Greenwillow/London: Julia MacRae.

Williams, V. (1983). *Something Special For Me*. New York: Greenwillow/London: Julia MacRae.

Williams, V. (1984). *Music, Music for Everyone*. New York. Greenwillow/London: Julia MacRae.

Williams, V. (1990). *'More, More, More!' Said the Baby*. New York: Greenwillow.

3 Reading against racism in South Africa

DENISE NEWFIELD

Context and educational infrastructure

It is not easy to write about South African society during this time of transition, this time of hope and despair, achievement and tragedy, cooperation and discord. It is difficult not to be cowed into silence by the magnitude of the events, in particular the carnage that has become almost a daily occurrence. Moreover, the situation changes so rapidly that events overtake their description. Writing about the sensitive and crucial issue of racism is particularly difficult in this interregnum as, all about us, rampantly racist behaviour is evident, even though anti-racism has ostensibly become hegemonic. It is therefore in a spirit of humility that I offer a few ideas on reading against racism in South Africa.

Before doing so, it is necessary to consider the educational system in this country as it still exists in 1992, despite the changes that have already taken place and the envisaged changes. Since President F.W. de Klerk's 'Address to the Nation' and the release of Nelson Mandela in February 1990, the infamous Population Registration Act and the Group Areas Act have been repealed, but the National Education Policy Act of 1967 has not. The contrasts between white affluence and black poverty, between the voting powers of whites and the disenfranchisement of blacks, remains. The characteristic images of green tree-lined white suburbs and drab black townships and depleted rural areas are clichéd but still accurate representations of South African life. The ideology of race that was carefully implemented by the Nationalist Government from 1948, and developed over four decades by a formidable array of apartheid legislation controlling, among other aspects of everyday life, place of residence, medical care, labour practice and schooling, has been officially revoked, but its effects remain much in evidence. Educational segregation remains firmly in place, with the exception of a few progressive[1] private schools, and a slow move by a small number of white state schools to admit carefully selected black students.[2] A summary of educational segregation in this country, published in 1990, still holds true:

There are 17 departments of education in South Africa. Black education outside the bantustans (the so-called independent states) is under the control of the Department of Education and Training (DET). There are separate departments for 'Coloureds' (people of mixed race) and Indians (people of Asian origin). White education is controlled by four separate departments, one for each of the four provinces in South Africa (Cape, Natal, Transvaal, and Orange Free State). In addition to these seven departments of education, there is a department for each of the bantustans: KaNgwane, Gazankulu, Lebowa, KwaNdebele, KwaZulu, QwaQwa, Ciskei, Transkei, Bophuthatswana and Venda.

(Janks, 1990: 242–3)

Different groups constructed on the basis of race (including tribal-regional factors and in some instances language) still go to different schools, have different syllabuses,[3] write different examinations, have different teachers (with different qualifications), and different material conditions in which to learn, though all under the eye of Big Brother, the state. To take just two examples, expenditure on white education has far exceeded expenditure on black education, allowing for the development of media centres, playing fields and swimming pools in white schools, whereas most black schools have none of these. The pupil–teacher ratios continue to differ widely in black and white schools.[4] Racism as an ideology continues to flourish in this context, and no matter how hard individual progressive teachers may attempt to help their students to 'read against racism', they are unlikely to succeed more than partially. I therefore wish to stress that the eradication of racism in education in South Africa depends on the eradication of racism in the social, economic and political spheres. This does not mean, however, that educators should not address themselves urgently to the tasks of endeavouring to restructure the educational system, to recreate the syllabi and curricula, to reselect setworks and textbooks in terms of new criteria, and to recommend new methodological approaches for the education of the future. Reading against racism in South Africa requires a holistic approach on the part of educators and teachers, as well as courage in the face of setbacks.

Curriculum and methodology

Despite the rigid segregation and the difference in level and quality of education between some of the different departments, the official selection of texts has revealed a uniformly hegemonic and Eurocentric bias which may be regarded, in the present South African context, as racist. This bias has been well documented by Jane Reid in her critical examination of setbooks in South African senior schools. Reid (1982) reveals that the literature setbook selection has been made largely according to the criterion of the elitist and Eurocentric notion of high culture, as well as strict Calvinist principles and a discriminatory notion of vocational training. Shakespeare, Dickens, Hardy, Wordsworth and so on have formed the staple core of English authors for all departmental curricula, with the result that schoolchildren have explored – often battled with – the landscapes of remote places and the sentiments of culturally remote peoples. This has tended to devalue both the black and the white students' sense of their own worth and of the worth of the country, resulting in a feeling of inferiority. As Reid put it so aptly, 'Daffodils and red roses are what the poets write about, so why bother to look at the cosmos?' There is little doubt that education departments in South Africa have kept students away from the literature of their own country:

> The reason for this decision is obvious. Much of the literature published in recent times by both black and white writers has been 'political'. Authors have portrayed again and again the hardships and injustices suffered by South Africans under the oppressive apartheid system. Three taboo subjects in South African schools are sex, politics and religion, and literature which deals too explicitly with these topics is considered suspect. The study of elitist British high culture protects us from having to focus on the terrifying problems of the world in which we live.
>
> (Janks and Paton, 1991: 227)

Even though some progress has been made in regard to indigenous literature in recent years in the white education departments, little has been made in other education departments. In 1986, black matriculants had to choose two out of the following setworks for their Department of Education and Training (DET) matriculation examination: (1) *Julius Caesar*, (2) *Richard the Third*, (3) Fitzgerald's *The Great Gatsby*, (4) Steinbeck's *The Pearl*, (5) a selection of modern short stories and (6) a selection of poems (only Serote's 'City Johannesburg' was South African). In 1990, DET students had to choose two of the following setworks: (1) *Romeo and Juliet*, (2) *I Heard The Owl Call My Name* by M. Craven (3) a selection of poems from *The Wind At Dawn* (a few are South African) and (4) a list of South African short stories from *Close to the Sun*.

Courageous and insightful teachers are able to teach, for example, the Shakespeares (which are overwhelmingly the most popular choice from these lists) in such a way as to make the process instructive and enjoyable for South African pupils.[5] However, the selection of setworks throughout the official curricula has failed to take cognisance of the fact that South Africa is part of Africa, and, until very recently, that black writers have contributed to the South African literary tradition. It has therefore failed to militate against the racism engendered in the education system as a whole. In fact, given the educational infrastructure, the ostrich mentality of many white schoolchildren up until now and the force of the Eurocentric tradition, the isolated South African texts included in some of the setwork lists have occasionally served to reinforce existing prejudices. In white schools, South

African texts have sometimes been met with a groan (a moralizing approach to racial issues on the part of well-meaning liberal teachers can, in certain contexts, make South African literature a non-starter), while in black schools the South African texts selected have been ostensibly apolitical and have not been well received judging by the relatively small number of candidates who select the South African short stories for their matriculation examination.

Changes are in sight, even officially. These changes involve more than the syllabus. In a controversial and heavily criticized move in 1990, the Minister of Education announced to white state schools the option of opening their doors to all races. The schools' future complexion would depend upon a complicated voting system involving the parents and teachers. Privatization, or partial privatization, would also be possible. No significant progress in terms of the population as a whole has been made.

More far-reaching are the changes outlined in the Education Renewal Strategy (ERS) document of June 1991, put out by the Department of National Education. A marked shift in discourse is apparent, by comparison with that in earlier official educational documents:

> It is recommended that race should not feature in structuring the provision of education in a future education model for South Africa and that justice in educational opportunities must be ensured.

While the 'strategy' outlined in the ERS document is broad-ranging, having profound implications for the education of all South Africans, the document's reception should be noted. The University of the Witwatersrand, for example, has stated that the document reflects the opinions, wishes and assumptions of the present bureaucracies rather than of the people of South Africa. As an imposition from above, the university believes that the ERS document lacks legitimacy.

Unofficially, developments sych as 'alternative education' or 'education for liberation' or 'people's education' have in recent years contested existing practices. Alternative groups have devised syllabuses, curricula and teaching materials in an attempt to redress the educational imbalance, to counteract the Eurocentric bias and to re-empower black learners. Foremost among these have been SACHED, an educational trust offering alternative materials, courses and distance learning, and People's Education is a Philosophy, which grew out of the National Education Crisis Committee at the end of 1985. People's Education is non-racial and democratic in scope and intention, a long-term 'mass-based undertaking by a whole society to transform itself' (Gardiner, 1987).

What has been called 'People's English' aims to assist all learners:

• to understand the evils of apartheid and to think and speak in non-racist, non-sexist and non-elitist ways;
• to determine their own destinies and free themselves from oppression;

- to play a creative role in the achievement of a non-racial democratic South Africa; . . .
- to express and consider the issues and questions of their time;
- to transform themselves into full and active members of their society.

(NEC Committee, 1990: 1)

The methods proposed by the People's English Commission are:

> . . . discussion, debate, argument, speeches; group and pair work; sharing and pooling of ideas; collecting and recording community-based experiences; the telling and retelling of stories; community participation; research, dramatization; performance and song; co-operation not competition; collective development not individualistic selfishness; thinking not memorising. Learners should also gain experience of the processes of production. They should design and produce newsletters, pamphlets, notices and posters. People's English believes alternative methods to be as important as if not more important than, alternative content.

(Janks, 1990: 257)

Mention must be made also of the projects currently being undertaken by the National Education Policy Investigation (NEPI), a commission organized under the auspices of the National Education Co-ordinating Committee (NECC) and university-based education policy units. NEPI is undertaking wide-ranging research into education with a view to presenting policy options for the future. Its core principles, as stated in an unpublished working document, are: non-racism, non-sexism, democracy, a unitary education system and redressing of historical imbalances. Its language policy research group is primarily concerned with language as medium of instruction and language as subject within a multilingual context, and is examining other issues such as the centrality of language within the English curriculum, textbooks, the problems faced by bilingual learners and teacher training.

Texts

In relation to racist texts, method is indeed important. If reading against racism is taken in its verbal sense (i.e. 'how to read against racist texts'), the method of oppositional reading becomes crucial. Although the literary tradition in English in South Africa has been, in the main, liberal, students do encounter colonial novels such as those by R.M. Ballantyne, Henry Rider Haggard and John Buchan. Departmental stockrooms had sets of these novels during the 1950s and 1960s (and possibly still do); however, they were read and studied uncritically. Buoyed along by the adventure and the often unrecognizably exotic South African settings, few teachers asked their students to consider the colonialist paternalism expressed in these novels in a critical light. As far as the Transvaal Education Department was concerned, *Coral Island, King Solomon's Mines* and *Prester John* presumably accorded with the prescribed educational philosophy of the time. There is no apparent conflict between the view of English rule expressed by Davie in *Prester John*, with which we are expected to agree, and that of the official policy of Christian National Education, still in force today, as expressed in Article 15 of its pamphlet of 1948 (the year the Nationalist Government came into power):

> I knew then the meaning of the white man's duty. He has to take all the risks ... That is the difference between white and black, the gift of respons-ibility, the power of being in a little way a king, and so long as we know it and then practise it, we will rule not in Africa alone but wherever there are dark men who live only for their bellies.
>
> (Buchan, 1910: 88)
>
> We believe that the calling and task of white South Africa with regard to the native is to Christianise him and help him on culturally, and that this calling and the task has already found its nearer focussing in the principles of trustee-ship, no equality and segregation ... On the grounds of the cultural infancy of the native, we believe that it is the right and task of the state ... to give and control native education.
>
> (Rose and Tunmer, 1975: 127–8)

Clearly, it is important to read such texts oppositionally, to discuss the racist and imperialist prejudices they contain, to put them into an histor-ical perspective, and to reveal whose interests are served by the attitudes informing the texts. Such an approach, which is the basis of Brian Street's (1975) reading of *King Solomon's Mines* in his study of 'the savage in litera-ture', reveals how Haggard's notion of race is informed by anthropolog-ical theory of the time and by notions of British imperialism. An oppositional approach should reveal to students Haggard's hierarchy of races, his view of the Englishman's role abroad, and his view of Africa as 'primitive'. Although Allan Quatermain, Haggard's narrator, is sympathetic to the 'natives', and not overtly racist, in the end his views are segregationist, as we see in the outcome of the love affair between Foulata and Captain Good, one of the three English travellers. Quatermain does not consider inter-racial marriage feasible. He sees taking Foulata back to England as problematic. This poten-tial problem is, however, overcome by the facile resolution of plot provided by Haggard: Foulata dies at the hand of Gagool the Witch while trying to save Captain Good. Her dying words to Quatermain are:

> Say to my lord ... that I love him, and that I am glad to die because I know he cannot cumber his life with such as I am, for the sun may not mate with the darkness, nor the white with the black.
>
> (Haggard, 1885: 260–1)

To encourage an oppositional reading of *King Solomon's Mines*, William Plomer's novella *Turbott Wolfe* may be fruitfully juxtaposed with it. *Turbott Wolfe*, as Plomer said, is a 'violent ejaculation', a protest against the racial prejudice he encountered during his sojourn in South Africa. The novella is set in the colonial trading station of Ovuzane near Aucampstroom during the 1920s. The major concern of the novel is expressed by Mabel van der Horst in her indignant reply to the missionary, Friston:

> You take away the black man's country, and, shirking the future consequences of your action, you blindly affix a label to what you know (and fear) the black man is thinking of you – 'the native question'. Native question, indeed! My good man, there is no native question. It isn't a question. It's an answer. I don't know whether people are wilfully blind, that they can't see what's coming. The white man's as dead as a doornail in this country... All this Empire-building's a blooming blind alley.
>
> (Plomer, 1926: 65–6)

The 'answer' is provided, rather shockingly, by a movement for the regeneration of South Africa:

> To put it in a Nutshell, WE BELIEVE:
> 1 That Africa is not the white man's country.
> 2 *That miscegenation is the only way for Africa to be secured to the Africans.*
> 3 That it is inevitable, right and proper.
> 4 That if it can be shown to be so, we shall have laid true foundations for the future coloured world.
>
> (ibid.: 70)

Alternatively, *King Solomon's Mines* may be read alongside Mphahlele's *Down Second Avenue*, an autobiographical account by a black writer of his early years. As an act of self-definition and self-knowledge, it refutes the stereotypical portrayal of blacks that informs the colonial-romance novel of Africa and that Mphahlele himself believes informs even that hugely popular liberal novel of the 1940s, *Cry, The Beloved Country*, by Alan Paton. Mphahlele objects to Paton's mode of characterization as 'flat' and manipulative:

> The Reverend Stephen Kumalo can be summed up by 'so in my suffering I can believe'. Msimangu, Paton's commentator ... can be summed up by: 'It is the law, Mother. We must uphold the law ... '. Kumalo also remains the same suffering Christlike, childlike character from beginning to end. He is always trembling with humility. He accepts the scheme of things ... He is always bewildered. Even after his bitter experiences in the city, he can still address the white boy from Jarvis' farm as 'inkosana' – little master ... Paton has thought fit to use this type for Kumalo's role for highly sentimental reasons. In the midst of so much pain, fear and dishonesty, he seems to say: 'Here is a man who does not hate, who harbors no bitterness. And he is a black man, too, one of a race that is often despised'.
>
> (Mphahlele, 1974: 157–8)

Questions on the discourse of texts such as these may be discussed among students in order to challenge their racism or paternalism. The following questions are suggested: Who is the narrator of the story? Who does he represent and where does he come from? To whom is he telling the story? What are the assumptions about race in the text? Whose interests are being served? Who is dominant and who is subordinate in the text? What terminology is used? Is it racist? What are the 'silences' of the text, i.e. what has been omitted? Are the metaphors culturally loaded? Whose values are assumed, i.e. taken as natural? Are they natural, a fact of life? Consider the closure/resolution of plot: what message does it convey? what ideological position does it reveal? (adapted from Janks, 1988: appendix A).

Reading against racism also involves the reading of texts that are in themselves anti-racist. South Africa has a strongly developed tradition of such texts. It is a commonplace that much South African English literature up to now has been a literature of resistance to apartheid. This field is so extensively developed that I can do no more than discuss a few examples, selected from the genre of contemporary poetry, since poetry has yielded a rich harvest of anti-racist writing by authors of all races over the past two decades.[6] Of the poetry of black writers, Michael Chapman (1982: 11 and 23) said:

> Soweto poetry[7] began appearing in the mid-1960s mainly in the Johannesburg-based literary magazine *The Classic* ... The work of poets such as Oswald Mtshali, Mongane Serote, Sipho Sepamla and Mafika Gwala took its impetus initially from South African student (SASO) Black Consciousness reactions to apartheid legislation, and subsequently from the 1976 Soweto disturbances. Theirs is a poetry which has been instrumental not only in re-establishing a vital tradition of black writing in South Africa, but in prompting serious, often uncomfortable, re-examination by writers and critics alike on the function of, and the appropriate responses to, literature in a racially turbulent society ... If Soweto poetry is regarded with some trepidation by the South African authorities as a potential instrument of social change (witness, for instance, the bannings of individual collections by Matthews, Sepamla, Madingoane and Mtshali, of single issues of Staffrider and of writers' groups like Medupe), then Soweto poetry has no less proved to be a dynamic instrument of literary change. It is a poetry which over the last ten years had boldly taken a Eurocentric South African Literary Establishment by the scruff of the neck and dragged it into an arena robustly and challengingly South African.

There is no doubt that the poetry of black writers rejuvenated South African poetry as a whole.

A challenging and accomplished South African poem which encapsulates the struggle against racism in this country, and from which I have taken the title of this chapter, is Jeremy Cronin's untitled piece:

To learn how to speak
With the voices of the land,
To parse the speech in its rivers,
To catch in the inarticulate grunt,
Stammer, call, cry, babble, tongue's knot
A sense of the stoneness of these stones
From which all words are cut.

To trace with the tongue wagon-trails
Saying the suffix of their aches in -kuil,* -pan,* -fontein,*
In watery names that confirm
The dryness of their ways.
To visit the places of occlusion, or the lick
in a vlei-bank* dawn.
To bury my mouth in the pit of your arm,
In that planetarium,
Pectoral beginning to the nub of time
Down there close to the water-table, to feel
The full moon as it drums
At the back of my throat
Its cow-skinned vowel.
To write a poem with words like:
I'm telling you,
Stompie,* stickfast,* golovan,*
Songololo,* just boombang,* just
To understand the least inflections,
To voice without swallowing
Syllables born in tin shacks, or catch
the 5.15 ikwata bust fife
Chwannisberg train, to reach
The low chant of the mine gang's
Mineral glow of our people's unbreakable resolve.

To learn how to speak
With the voices of this land.

(Cronin, 1983: 58)

*kuil	Afrikaans word meaning pool or waterhole, often found in place-names
pan	Afrikaans word meaning circular depression in which water accumulates after it has rained
fontein	Afrikaans word meaning spring or fountain. Cronin uses these suffixes ironically since their 'watery names' are at odds with the frequently dry climatic conditions of the places they designate. Taken in conjunction with 'wagon-trails' of the previous line, the words evoke a sense of South African history as well as geography
vlei	Afrikaans word meaning lake or swamp
stompie	word of Afrikaans origin, now a much used South African slang term for cigarette butt
stickfast	'to stick fast' is a South African colloquial expression meaning to get stuck, usually while travelling, but not always
golovan	a word used by miners for cocopan to refer to the small tip-truck for transporting ore
songololo	a word of Nguni origin for millipede
boombang	a colloquial South African expression meaning fast or 'just like that')

It is a poem which stands for non-racism, inclusivity, integration, synthesis, solidarity, liberation. The poem is a plea for the acceptance of difference, without discrimination, and Hopkins-like, a paean to the richness of diversity but rooted in the premise that liberty is indivisible. It is clearly South African in its setting, geographical metaphors and dialect, but its message can be appreciated by multicultural societies all over the globe.

The poem is structured as a prayer, the articulation of a longing. The poet longs for that gift of language that will enable him to express the seemingly inexpressible, to give voice to those in South Africa with no voice. Included in the latter group, but not in any way foregrounded or made explicit ('I' is noticeably absent in the text), is the poet himself, silenced in prison. A major difficulty in speaking with 'the voices of the land' lies in the problem of verbalization *per se*, as the poem's opening lines indicate. Blending literal and metaphoric levels of language, these lines evoke a sense of language struggling to articulate South African history and geography accurately. Paradoxically, rivers have 'speech', while the poet has 'to learn how to speak' and to understand speech, to 'parse'. 'Grunt,/Stammer, call, cry, babble, tongue's knot' evokes the struggle towards linguistic articulation and the political struggle. 'To trace with the tongue wagon-trails' renders the move-ment of the tongue in the mouth as well as the journey inland of the Trek-boers during the nineteenth century. In the central section of the poem, the longing becomes physical, sexual. Implied in the text is the loss of physical and social contact endured by the prisoner in solitary confinement and others, such as migrant workers, who are separated from kith and kin.

The final section of the poem (beginning with 'To write . . .') concerns itself with the writing of poetry. The poet's wish to be able to express every-day South African speech constitutes an implicit rejection of 'elevated' diction and Standard English as the natural language of poetry. The Afrikanerisms, Africanisms and slang are expressions of living culture and attempt to capture the variety and nuances in a multilingual society. The accented rendering of the 5.15 Johannesburg train and the compression of 'syllables born in tin shacks' vividly evoke the lives of black people commut-ing daily to the workplace from their makeshift homes in the townships or squatter camps. The final lines of this section nullify racial, class and social barriers, as exemplified in the inclusive pronoun 'our'. The 'mine gang's mineral glow' expresses the 'unbreakable resolve' of 'our people'. Poet, miners, all South Africans, are one. The poem's achievement is to have encapsulated not only many of South Africa's communities and characteristic situations, its paradoxical landscape and the burden of its history, but also the poet's personal yet simultaneously representative aspiration for fellow-ship and freedom. To these Cronin has given voice in a poem of subtlety, wit and passion.

Cronin is an interesting poet to study within the context of racism, since both his work and his life exemplify a transcendence of it. He was born in

1949, the son of an officer in the South African Navy. His life has been characterized by an attempt to change the nature of society in South Africa. He has fought consistently against apartheid. As an academic, among other endeavours, he has sought to broaden the confining parameters of English literature in this country, and as a poet, he has studied and been influenced by indigenous oral traditions. In 1976, he was sentenced to 7 years' imprisonment for carrying out underground work for the then outlawed African National Congress (ANC), of which 3 years were spent alongside death row prisoners in the Pretoria maximum security jail. The title of his anthology, *Inside*, published in 1983 soon after his release, refers to his incarceration and to his thoughts, feelings and experiences during that period.

'To learn how to speak' can be studied in the literature classroom as:

1 An expression of belief in the universal dignity of humankind irrespective of race.
2 A literary production arising out of deleterious material conditions.
3 An attempt to blend the Western and indigenous poetic traditions.
4 An articulation partially in South African dialect.
5 As a rallying call within South Africa to all its peoples.

It is thus highly suitable for inclusion in secondary school syllabuses. Questions put to students on the language issue could include: To whom does the poet wish to speak? Which language(s) does he select and why? (This introduces the issue of English as a common language in preference to Afrikaans, considered by many to be the language of the oppressor;[8] English as the language of access to education and commerce; also Englishes in South Africa as opposed to standard English.) What is the difference between 'voices' and languages, and how many languages and voices are heard in the poem?

Another anti-racist poem by Cronin revealing the sense of solidarity between the white poet-prisoner and a fellow black prisoner, both in solitary confinement, is 'Motho Ke Motho Ka Batho Babang' (a Sotho proverb meaning 'a person is a person because of other people'). The black prisoner speaks to Cronin in sign language and warns him of the presence of a warder. Once again language is important in this poem. Afrikaans is the language of the prison authorities: 'Hey, Wat maak jy daar?' (Hey! What are you doing?) and 'baas' (boss), whereas in the struggle for freedom, black and white prisoners, speakers of any language, are united.

Motho Ke Motho Ka Batho Babang
(A person is a person because of other people)

By holding my mirror out of the window I see
Clear to the end of the passage.
There's a person down there.
A prisoner polishing a doorhandle.
In the mirror I see him see
My face in the mirror,

I see the fingertips of his free hand
Bunch together, as if to make
An object the size of a badge
Which travels up to his forehead
The place of an imaginary cap.
(This means: A *warder*).
Two fingers are extended in a vee
And wiggle like two antennae.
(He's being watched).
A finger of his free hand makes a watch-hand's arc
On the wrist of his polishing arm without
Disrupting the slow-slow rhythm of his work.
(*Later*. Maybe, later we can speak).
Hey! Wat maak jy daar?
– a voice from around the corner.
No. Just polishing baas.
He turns his back to me, now watch
His free hand, the talkative one,
Slips quietly behind
– *Strength brother*, it says,
In my mirror,
A black fist.

(Cronin, 1983: 15)

'Death Row' is another poem by Cronin about Pretoria Central Prison showing a cultural and political unity that transcends race. Its strongly aural
qualities make it a superb choice for choral verse at secondary school level.

Placing short poems by Mongane Serote and James Matthews in juxta-
position with a poem by Douglas Livingstone is instructive, for the exercise
shows clearly how the different living conditions in black and white communities have given rise to different poetic concerns and styles. In 'The
Earthshaker', Douglas Livingstone explores the season of spring in a South
African application of the traditional theme, whereas James Matthews, in
language bare of decoration and description, states his inability to concern
himself with the beauties of nature:

The Earthshaker

One hot still late afternoon
when the first pedantic and altogether
surprising bee
rumbles up fussily to the swooned
open mouth of a cornucopia,
self-contained but unwarily
clowning his heraldic role with a pompous
booming and bumbling,
backing and filling testily
to clear a throat of stinging sweetness

and stops headdown,
intent, thirstily –

His greedy silence magic –
carpets in the tiny advance
of sounds over grass,
the hand over hand heady climb past
the thorn to the rosebud
as Spring launches its assault.

Tonight for the first time
in centuries it will be:
blankets on the lawn, chilled wine
and cigarettes, the moon through the
nets of silver-new
creeper-rose, and you;
and the search on the once-parched
meadows of your mouth
for the wellsprings of dew.

                (Livingstone, 1964: 26)

i wish i could write a
poem
record the beginning of
dawn
the opening of a flower
at the approach of a bee
describe a bird's first flight
then i look at people
maimed, shackled, jailed,
the knowing is now clear
i will never be able to write
a poem about dawn, a bird or a
bee

           (Matthews, 1981: 1)

Mongane Serote, in a poem from which André Brink took the title of his novel, writes of a dry, white and barren time:

For Don M. – Banned

it is a dry white season
dark leaves don't last, their brief lives dry out
they dive down gently headed for the earth
not even bleeding.
it is a dry white season brother,
only the trees know the pain as they still stand erect

dry like steel, their branches dry like wire,
indeed, it is a dry white season
but seasons come to pass.

(Serote, 1981: 341)

I believe it is essential to place our different poetic traditions side by side, contextualizing each, in order for our pupils to explore both European and African poetic traditions, and in order to acquire an understanding of South African and European culture.

'Sea and Sand' by Don Mattera (addressee in the previous poem) is a poem which may at first sight seem to advocate racism, discrimination against whites. The poem actually attempts to redress the discrimination against black people that has existed for so long in this country. Mattera's standpoint is rooted in the philosophy of Black Consciousness, which was developed by black South Africans towards the end of the 1960s. In his book *I Write What I Like*, Steve Biko commented on Black Consciousness as follows: 'Merely by describing yourself as black you have started on a road towards emancipation, you have committed yourself to fight against all forces that seek to use your blackness as a stamp that marks you out as a subservient being.' Mattera's poem wittily and movingly extends this idea.

Sea and Sand

Sea and sand
My love
My land,
   God bless Africa
Sea and sand
My love
My land,
   God bless Africa
   But more the South of Africa
   Where we live . . .
Bless the angry mountains
And the smiling hills
Where the cool water spills
To heal the earth's brow

Bless the children of South Africa
The white children
And the black children
   But more the black children
   Who lost the sea and the sand
   That they may not lose love
   For white children
   Whose fathers raped the land . . .

Sea and sand
My love, my land,
God bless Africa . . .
                    (Mattera, 1983: 58)

Don Mattera is a South African writer, journalist, speaker and community leader. When younger, he was a footballer and gang leader. He was banned during the 1970s. His grandfather was Italian and his mother African, and therefore the South African authorities classified him as 'Coloured' in accordance with their criterion of mixed race.

Robert Miles has discussed the way in which the classification of people into different groups gives rise to racism. In his book *Racism*, he states:

> I argue that racism 'works' by attributing meanings to certain phenotypical and/or genetic characteristics of human beings in such a way as to create a system of categorization, and by attributing additional (negatively evaluated) characteristics to the people sorted into these categories. This process of signification is therefore the basis for the creation of a hierarchy of groups, and for establishing criteria by which to include and exclude groups of people in the process of allocating resources and services.
>
>   (Miles, 1989: 3)

A news report in a Johannesburg newspaper a few years ago is interesting to examine in the light of Miles's argument. It has been included in a recent poetry anthology as a 'Concrete Poem', presumably because it was felt that reportage of the list of facts constituted an absurdity that was almost poetic. Written by the newspaper's political staff, the true author of the piece is Stoffel Botha, the Minister of Home Affairs, drawing his inspiration from the racial laws of South Africa, as they existed in 1985 (the Population Registration Act was repealed in 1991). The absurdity of these laws is instantly recognized, as is the arbitrariness of race classification *per se*.

I would like to consider this news report as a literary text, which even though 'factual' appears to be 'fictional'. In its own zany way, the text exhibits the compression and intensity of poetry. Its complexity of tone and formal features make it seem closer to literary discourse than to journalism. In addition, the choice of this text in a literature classroom raises the question of what counts as literature and who decides.

1985 had at least 1000 'chameleons'
by Political Staff

PARLIAMENT – More than 1000 people officially changed colour last year.

They were reclassified from one race group to another by the stroke of a Government pen.

Details of what is dubbed 'the chameleon dance' were given in reply to Opposition questions in Parliament.

The Minister of Home Affairs, Mr Stoffel Botha, disclosed that during 1985:

- 702 coloured people turned white.
- 19 whites became coloured.
- One Indian became white.
- Three Chinese became white.
- 50 Indians became coloured.
- 43 coloureds became Indians.
- 21 Indians became Malay.
- 30 Malays went Indian.
- 249 blacks became coloured.
- 20 coloureds became black.
- Two blacks became 'other Asians.'
- One black was classified Griqua.
- 11 coloureds became Chinese.
- Three coloureds went Malay.
- One Chinese became coloured.
- Eight Malays became coloured.
- Three blacks were classed as Malay.
- No blacks became white and no whites became black.

(*The Star*, Johannesburg, 21 March 1986)

It might be useful for students to examine this 'poem' critically, in relation to structure, tone and, of course, content. Students could be given questions to discuss in groups on the following aspects:

1 The significance of the headline/title.
2 The significance of the context, given as Parliament in the opening line, in relation to the piece as a whole. What was the constitution of this parliament at the given time, and what is it now?
3 The tone of the opening paragraphs. What does this tell you about the newspaper's editorial policy/ideological position?
4 Choice of verbs in the list of changes, e.g. 'turned', 'became', 'went'. Compare their usual meaning with the meaning here.
5 The effect of the list format, as opposed to the format of a conventional paragraph. Discussion should include the length of the list, repetition and variation.
6 Definitions of white, coloured, Indian, Chinese, Malay, blacks, 'other Asians', Griqua. Is this a difficult task? What conclusion can you draw?
7 The final item: 'No blacks became white and no whites became black'. Explain why.
8 Who or what classifies people into these different race groups? Are they different race groups? What *is* race?
9 To what extent is this text 'literature'. Is it a 'poem'?

A colleague of mine sometimes precedes a class on this news report/poem with exercises requiring pupils to consider the way different languages classify the world differently (e.g. the way English has fewer words for 'snow' than Eskimo, and South Sotho, a South African language, many more words for 'milk' than English), and also to consider 'what South Africa would like if people were grouped according to: (i) eye colour, (ii) blood type, (iii) shoe size, (iv) height, (v) hair colour'. She asks the students to try to work out who would dominate and to give reasons why (Janks, 1986: 1).

Among the other South African poems on the theme of non-racism that have impact in the classroom are 'Da Same, Da Same' and 'To Whom it may Concern' by Sidney Sepamla. Written in dialect, in a pseudo-naive tone, 'Da Same, Da Same' states its argument simply and succinctly, reaching a mythic dimension in its final stanza:

> sometimes you wanna know how I meaning for
> is simples
> when da nail of da t'orn[a] tree
> scratch little bit little bit of da skin
> I doesn't care of[b] say[c] black
> I doesn't care of say white
> I doesn't care of say India[d]
> I doesn't care of say kleeling[e]
> I mean for sure da skin
> only one t'ing[f] come for sure
> and da one t'ing for sure is red blood
> dats for sure da[g] same da same
> for avarybudy[h]
> (Sepamla, 1979: 219)

(*a* thorn; *b* if; *c* she/he; *d* Indian; *e* Coloured; *f* thing; *g* the; *h* everybody)

'To Whom it may Concern' deconstructs the traditional ethnic and religious divisions in South Africa and satirizes the now – but not then – partially revoked laws of domicile, travel and designation. The satiric point is clinched in the final lines, which refer to an ethno-religious grouping. Exposed as a subdivision of apartheid racial separatism, this grouping functions even after death. The reader is asked to note that when the poem's degraded, depersonalized protagonist, the 'Bantu', has completed his life's work (the insinuation of exploitation is clear), he will be buried in a plot for Methodist Xhosas,

> The remains of R/N 417181
> Will be laid to rest in peace
> On a plot
> Set aside for Methodist Xhosas
> A measure also adopted
> At the express request of the Bantu
> In anticipation of any faction fight
> Before the Day of Judgement
> (Sepamla, 1981)

The post-1976 period has seen the poetry of protest, which was often directed at a liberal white audience, give way to the poetry of assertion and resistance. In the latter, the racially oppressed, through the voice of the individual poet, assert their right to a liberated future and to their own aesthetic. James Matthews wrote the following poem in 1981 in a context of severe censorship of political activity as well as of other written genres. Resistance poetry was then, and still is, often performed in South Africa. It is more difficult to suppress the spoken than the written word.

> poems have
> become pistols
> balladeers now
> use songs
> to create
> political statements
> blood-splashed
> words/pain-flowers
> sprouting from
> ravaged flesh
> no time
> for dreams
>   (Mathews, 1981: 53)

Chris Van Wyk's poem 'About Graffiti' is a graphic though oblique depiction of racism from its opening lines (Western and Noordgesig are coloured townships):

> Graffiti is the writing on the wall
> the writing on the wall as at Western
>   'Heroes die young'
> In Noordgesig you'll see graffiti
> 'Why Lord can't we live together'

to its final assertion:

> Soon graffiti will wade into Jo'burg
> unhampered by the tourniquet of influx control
>   (Van Wyk, 1979: 13–15)

Given the nature and function of graffiti in relation to language and society, this poem is worth discussing in the English classroom, as is Van Wyk's 'In Detention', a bitter attack on the laws that have allowed detention without trial of political figures such as Ahmed Timol, Steven Biko and Neil Aggett, who are among those who died mysteriously while in detention:

> *In Detention*
>
> He fell from the ninth floor
> He hanged himself
> He slipped on a piece of soap while washing
> He hanged himself
> He slipped on a piece of soap while washing

He fell from the ninth floor
He hanged himself while washing
He slipped from the ninth floor
He hung from the ninth floor
He slipped on the ninth floor while washing
He fell from a piece of soap while slipping
He hung from the ninth floor
He washed from the ninth floor while slipping
He hung from a piece of soap while washing
                                    (Van Wyk, 1979: 45)

I conclude the poetry section with a very short piece from a collection of writings and drawings of children from the townships. The voice of black children who live in the townships but who have attended an extra-curricular cultural programme in the city is heard here, expressing their experiences of daily life. One of the tersest and most moving descriptions of racial inequality is that given by Moagi, aged 8, who says:

> When I am old I would like to have a wife and two children a boy and a girl and a big house and two dogs and freedom
>   (The Open School, 1986: 54–5)

I would like to conclude my chapter by moving away from the genre of poetry to popular literature that has been produced for readers in South Africa who have acquired only basic literacy. The material produced by the Storyteller Group has a dual aim, that of improving the competence of its second language readers and that of intervening in a reading environment that continues, by omission if not design, to reinforce the now officially dead apartheid ideology. The Storyteller Group aims to provide appropriate reading material for a non-racial, post-apartheid society, but one in which much rebuilding will still need to be done. The Group provides the following rationale of its work.

> South Africa is entering a most challenging and exciting era: an era of reconstruction, reconciliation, and redistribution, both of wealth and of power.
>
> A willingness is developing to redress the inequalities of the apartheid legacy; pragmatic realism is motivating what moral imperative could not.
>
> Ordinary South Africans, however, are caught in a spiral of fear and ignorance that effectively robs them of a vision of future possibilities.
>
> To break free of the apartheid chrysalis we need, above all, to boldly project images of 'what can be'.
>
> We need to 'pull' people with a vision of the future, not 'push' them with the guilt and resentment of the past.
>   (Napper and Esterhuysen, 1990: 14)

The project, devised primarily for disadvantaged black readers but also being used in 1991 in non-racial schools and about to be tested in white schools, has been concerned with the production of popular literature and with finding channels of distribution that would ensure a wide readership (by contrast with the relatively limited readership achieved by most of the literary texts mentioned so far in this chapter). According to Peter Esterhuysen, the Storyteller Group's effort has been as democratic as possible in terms of its selection of genre, its notion of audience, its 'bottom-up rather than top-down' approach to the creation of the texts and its response to feedback. The texts are created, for example, through interactive methods such as workshopping an idea with the children whose lives form the basis of the text. In its proposal for 'Effective Intervention', the Storyteller Group outlines its position. The promotion of reading, concern for the environment, and the theme of social reconstruction are all major ideals. Propagation of these ideals does not take the form of protest or strident assertion, but the matter-of-fact presentation of a non-racial world which is then naturalized. This world focuses primarily on the lives of black schoolchildren who have the desire, ability and opportunity to learn, to fulfil themselves as individuals and to make a positive contribution to their community. As Esterhuysen (1990) has said: 'Racism is not about hating blacks, but about presenting negative stereotypes of black people, often in a paternalistic way.' The Storyteller Group aims to provide black readers with a sense of dignity and worth, through presenting them as seen through their own eyes, and children of all colours with a sense that they can study and play together, as well as showing that South Africa, like Europe, is a place of stories. The stories, although neither prescriptive nor propagandistic, attempt to be 'a way of empowering people' (ibid.), which seems to me the essential component of the struggle against racism.

The comic is the genre which has been selected by the Storyteller Group. Given the aim of writing for a readership with limited language proficiency skills, the combination of words and pictures seemed appropriate within the ambit of contemporary popular literature. In 1991, the Storyteller Group has distributed 350 000 copies of a 22-page comic in the *99 Sharp Street* series. Called 'The River of Our Dreams', its plot revolves around a biology expedition to Natal by a group of Standard 6 students who live in Hillbrow, one of Johannesburg's 'grey' (i.e. mixed) areas. Among the main characters are the twins, Lebo and Veli Moeketsi, students at a new school called Stride Universal College, Thandi Cele, who lives with her grandfather on the top floor of a building called 99 Sharp Street, and her white friend, Alice Campbell, whom she has met at Marydale Convent.

In striving for authenticity of character, the writers have attempted authenticity of dialogue. Although the language of the comic is English, and, in the case of the comic's narration, Standard English, the dialogue contains a number of South Africanisms, including the exclamations 'Haai!' and 'Yo! Yo! Yo!', the epithet 'nca', the Afrikanerism "Heyta daar, my sister', and the streetwise slang 'sharp sharp', from which the comic's title is taken.

Thandi's grandfather uses the Zulu greeting 'Sawubona' when they arrive in Natal. All of this constitutes a naturalization of South African English as a major language among other existing languages, just as the use of the vernacular and of the African first names Veli, Lebo, Thandi and so on constitutes a valorization of Africa. This practice, in keeping with current naming practice in South Africa among blacks and even some whites, forms a contract with earlier South African literature which often employed anglicized or given English names for its African protagonists (e.g. Stephen Kumalo in *Cry, the Beloved Country*).

'The River of Our Dreams' does indeed record, to use Cronin's phrasing, many of 'the voices of the land': the ceremonial Zulu of the adults; the colloquial English of the students; the formal, scientific English of the biology textbook; the epistolary register of the friendly letter from Phumi to Lebo; the traditional tenor of the Zulu proverb; the 'rap' song about river pollution on the back cover; the précis form on the dramatis personae page. This rich diversity of language usage makes the comic a useful instructional model for English learners inside or outside the classroom.

An Afrocentric perspective is evident also in the representation of indigenous artists as part of the comic's milieu. Lebo's favourite musician is Ray Phiri, and Phumi is reading a book by Bessie Head, a South African writer who went into exile in Botswana. Thandi's grandfather sings a song 'composed by the famous guitarist, John Bhengu'. Veli is called 'the People's Poet', and allusion to the popular current practice of performance poetry exemplified by the political poetry of Mzwakhe Mbuli:

Oh, river, once a beautiful, flowing dream
Now a dark and muddy nightmare.

Tribal beliefs, though not featuring prominently, are part of the worldview of the comic (Thandi's grandfather hears his ancestors calling), as is African history. Thandi's grandfather (nicknamed the General) answers the headmaster's question about his participation in the Second World War in the affirmative: 'Yes, I fought in Italy'.

The comic's narrative leads up to the students' discovery of the filthy river running through the Natal village where they are to set up camp: '[The] river is a dump . . . Nothing could live in this river.' The visiting students decide to clean up the debris littering its banks. They form an action group, which is supported by the teachers and the local community. The comic ends with the process of cleaning only half-completed. The tour bus is heading towards the factory whose chemical emissions have polluted the water of the river. The headmaster's words provide a fitting closure to this part of the story, implying a sequel: 'What a successful trip!' he says. 'But this is only the beginning. Class, I had another dream last night . . .'.

The river acquires a strongly symbolic connotation. Taken in conjunction with the discussion on violence between Thandi's grandfather and the local teacher ('Our children have suffered enough. The time is ripe for a new South Africa'), the river of dreams comes to stand for the archetypal voyage of self-discovery, not merely of the individual but of a people. As stated in StoryNet, the newsletter of the Research Project of the Storyteller Group, 'The River of Our Dreams' has three main thematic strands: 'the way in which reading can enrich our lives, the importance of caring for our environment, and the need for communities to rebuild grassroots structures . . . the way in which people in oppressed communities take charge of their lives'.

The many responses to the first instalments of 99 Sharp Street indicate the enthusiasm with which this project has been received by educators and, more importantly, by readers. A few extracts from some of the letters are provided:

> Teacher, Mbhundule School
> The story is interesting and educational and it reveals the image of our modern life and environment.
>
> Petros Hlongwa
> The story give me a good idea. Because this story talk about the life of the township so I like so much and the pictures too. The most thing I like in language and pictures. Sorry for poor English I'm African boy.
>
> L.M. Phala
> What you issued us in this magazine slowly and surely it will build up the nation.
>
> (Napper and Esterhuysen, 1990: appendix 2)

In its project to develop popular visual material, the Storyteller Group has completed work on other Sharp Street stories and developed plot scenarios for three other comics. The Jazz Room is a dramatization of the vital 1950s era of South African township culture as seen through the eyes of musicians, singers, journalists and gangsters. Chippa and the Dribbling Wizards explores the conflict and excitement of South Africa's most popular sport, football. Golden City Dreams exposes the tensions between the private world and the public face of the South African music industry. The stories not only reflect the realities and aspirations of their readers' lives, but also show how ordinary people and communities can overcome adversity. These three projects show, I believe, a critical attitude to the past and present, as well as an overall spirit of optimism. The Jazz Room reconstructs history (most official history books that students would encounter in school would not even mention the lively but doomed culture of the 1950s), while Chippa and Golden City Dreams provide an analytical view of the present.

I have proposed the following methods of reading against racism in this chapter: critical or oppositional reading of overtly or covertly racist texts, reading of texts that are in themselves anti-racist, and the promotion of reading skills through texts that reconstruct in literature a new present. In closing my overview of reading against racism in South Africa with the work of the Storyteller Group, I wish to stress the dual themes of reconstruction *in* literature and reconstruction *through* literature, which seem to me an important, even if limited, part of the anti-racist effort in South Africa in this time of flux and anticipation. I also wish to stress the importance of indigenous, non-racist and popular material as a necessary complement to the traditional, great literary texts that form the staple diet of English courses all over the world.

Author's note (March 1991)

In view of the changing circumstances in South Africa, I wish to report that the following discriminatory laws (among others) remain on the statute books in March 1992 (*Source*: Evans, 1991):

1 Republic of South Africa Constitution Act of 1983 (legislative basis for the Tricameral Parliament and all that falls under its ambit, e.g. racially separate government departments, by-elections and referendums, and the exclusion of Blacks from Parliament).
2 Electoral Act of 1979 (separate franchise for Whites, Coloureds and Indians. No franchise for Blacks).
3 National States Citizenship Act of 1970 (its consequences have only been mitigated by the Restoration of South African Citizenship Act of 1986).
4 Black Administration Act of 1927 (gives power to the state president to depose tribal chiefs).
5 National Education Policy Act of 1967 (racially separate education departments).
6 General Pensions Act of 1979 (differential pensions for different racial groups).
7 Defense Act of 1957 (whites-only conscription).

Notes

1 'Progressive' is an umbrella term that has gained currency over the past few years. It refers to people (or institutions) on the left who subscribe to, and are working towards, a non-racial, democratic South Africa. Here it refers to schools which offer non-racial, multicultural education, such as Woodmead, Sacred Heart or Barnato Park. The latter, one of Johannesburg's oldest schools for white girls, was closed recently on account of diminishing numbers. After a vigorous campaign spearheaded by ASAP (All Schools for All People), the school re-opened as a mixed-sex, non-racial school.
2 These schools are permitted to do so in terms of the Model B option announced by Education Minister Piet Clase in October 1990.
3 Most of the so-called independent states, though having their own education departments, follow the DET matriculation English syllabus.
4 As given by the South African Institute of Race Relations, October 1990, the pupil/teacher ratios are: 16 to 1 in white schools and 50 to 1 in black schools.
5 An example is the method of free dramatization utilized by lecturers in English Education, University of the Witwatersrand, and documented in a video

programme, entitled *Teaching Shakespeare through Drama*, devised by Denise Newfield, produced by the Central Television Unit for the Department of English, University of the Witwatersrand, Johannesburg, 1987.

6 Black writers of the 1960s and 1970s turned to poetry rather than prose which had flourished in the 1950s. Oswald Mtshali, a black poet, remarked that 'a black man's life in South Africa is endlessly a series of poems . . . His is a poetic existence shaped by the harsh realities around him' (Chapman, 1982: 105). According to Nadine Gordimer, 'in the 1950s and early 60s prose writing by black South Africans was some of the best on the continent. Nearly all those seminal black writers went into exile in the sixties, and their works were banned . . . No fiction of any real quality has been written since then by a black writer still living in South Africa' (Gordimer, 1973: 51). She was of the opinion that had the black writers' 'subconscious search for a form less vulnerable than those forms that led a previous generation into banning and exile' led them into poetic rather than prose forms. N. Chabani Manganyi feels that 'poetry, and, to a lesser extent, the dramatic form appear to be the most appropriate mediums for creative individuals in the grip of an *experiential overload*' (Chapman, 1983: 148).

7 Michael Chapman's term 'Soweto poetry' has been heavily critized. The renaissance in black poety included a far wider range of poets than those from Soweto alone. As Mafika Gwala put it, 'I refuse to be called a "Soweto Poet" . . . I just cannot consider myself in the mould of a "Soweto Poet". Living with constant fear and bitter anger in this country does not revolve around Soweto alone. More, telling the world how my people are suffering and being hounded is more important than being a literary figure' (*Staffrider*, 8(1), 1989: 70).

8 However, the alternative Afrikaans movement spearheaded at the University of the Western Cape claims that Afrikaans is as much a language of the people as of the oppressor, since there are more 'coloured' Afrikaans speakers than white Afrikaans speakers. The alternative newspaper *Die Drye Weekblad* could be used as further evidence against a simplistic Afrikaans/oppression equation.

References

Biko, S. (1978). *I Write What I Like* (ed. Aelred Stubbs, C.R.). London: Heinemann.

Buchan, J. (1950). *Prester John*. London: Pan Books.

Chapman, M. (ed.) (1982). *Soweto Poetry*. Johannesburg: McGraw-Hill.

Cronin, J. (1983). *Inside*. Johannesburg: Ravan Press.

Esterhuysen P. (1990). An interview with Denise Newfield, Auckland Park, Johannesburg, October.

Evans, G. (1991). Apartheid is still alive and well on the statute books. *The Weekly Mail*, 23–29 August, p. 13.

Gardiner, M. (1987). Liberating language: People's English for the future. *Lengwitch*, 4(1), March: 36–40.

Gordimer, N. (1973). *The Black Interpreters*. Johannesburg: Sprocas-Ravan.

Haggard, H.R. (1885). *King Solomon's Mines*. London: Cassell.

Janks, H. (1986). Classifications are made not given. In *A Book about Language*, Vol. III. Johannesburg: Department of English, University of the Witwatersrand.

Janks, H. (1988). 'To catch a wake-up: Language awareness in the South African context'. Unpublished dissertation, University of the Witwatersrand, Johannesburg.

Janks, H. (1990). Contested terrain: English education in South Africa 1948–1987. In Goodson, I. and Medway, P. (eds), *Bringing English to Order*. London: Falmer Press.

Janks, H. and Paton, J. (1991). English and the teaching of English in South Africa. In Britton, J., Shafer, R. and Watson, K. (eds), *Teaching and Learning English Worldwide*. Clevedon.

Livingstone, D. (1964). The Earthshaker. In *Sjambok and Other Poems from Africa*. London: Oxford University Press.

Mattera, D. (1983). *Azanian Love Song*. Johannesburg: Skotaville.

Matthews, J. (1981). *No Time for Dreams*. Cape Town: BLAC Publishing.

Miles, R. (1989). *Racism*. London: Routledge.

Mphahlele, E. (1959). *Down Second Avenue*. London: Faber.

Mphahlele, E. (1974). *The African Image*. London: Faber and Faber.

Napper, N. and Esterhuysen, P. (1990). *Popular Literature*. Johannesburg: The Storyteller Group.

NEC (National Education Crisis) Committee (1990). People's English for people's power: Draft proposals. Press Release, 27 November.

The Open School (1986). *Two Dogs and Freedom*. Johannesburg: Ravan Press.

Paton, A. (1948). *Cry, The Beloved Country*. London: Jonathan Cape.

Plomer, W. (1926). *Turbott Wolfe*. Johannesburg: A.D. Donker.

Reid, J. (1982). *English Literature in South African Senior Schools*. Cape Town: Centre for African Studies, University of Cape Town.

Rose, B. and Tunmer, R. (1975). *Documents in South African Education*. Johannesburg: A.D. Donker.

Sepamla, S. (1979). Da Same, Da Same. In Butler, G. and Mann, C. (eds), *A New Book of South African Verse in English*. Cape Town: Oxford University Press.

Sepamla, S. (1981). To whom it may concern. In Butler, G. and Mann, C. (eds), *A New Book of South African Verse in English*. Cape Town: Oxford University Press.

Serote, M.W. (1981). For Don M. – Banned. In Chapman, M. (ed.), *A Century of South African Poetry*. Johannesburg: A.D. Donker.

Street, B.V. (1975). *The Savage in Literature*. London: Routledge and Kegan Paul.

Van Wyk, C. (1979). *It is Time to Go Home*. Johannesburg: A.D. Donker.

4 Mirror and springboard: An Australian teacher grows up

JIM KABLE

It has often been remarked that one's childhood is another country. And it *is* another country which we regularly and often subconsciously mine for contemporary meaning and then inevitably re-interpret in terms of the present.

Following the traumatic premature loss of my first child a couple of years ago, I found myself constructing a naively styled symbolic piece of art which traces my relations with, and understanding of, Koori Australia.[1] In one of the panels I show a small white boy taunting an equally small black boy with the epithet 'Blackie!' In the background, I have drawn a classroom. At the end of the verandah fronting this building is a tall cupboard, the door of which hangs slightly ajar. In this cupboard, I recall hiding when my victim justifiably chased me, seeking some physical retribution to counter my verbal humiliation of him. Of anything else which may have transpired I have no memory save that the other boy's name was Billy Munro. The year was 1955 and I cannot have long turned 6 years old.

This incident had skirted the edge of my consciousness for a long time, but it was one with which I did not directly deal until a decade ago. Initial shame gave way to an examination of the wider perspective of the society in which I was being reared. So, what was it like in Australia, 1955? For a start, Koori people were not citizens, were not counted in any census, were unable to vote, were frequently denied any but the most rudimentary educational opportunities, and had very little protection either from the law or by the law. It was a society in which most states had governmental bodies known by such ironic titles as the Aborigines Protection/Welfare Board. These were instruments of monumental oppression in controlling the lives of Koori people and were at their most iniquitous in the removal of children (toddlers upwards) from their families' care. Placed in institutions, they were trained to become domestic slaves (especially in the homes of the urban white middle class) if girls or farm slaves if boys. They suffered all sorts of abuse, the least of it being the paltry payment meted out if lucky – the 'lousy little sixpence' chronicled so movingly in the documentary film of that name. Organizations such as Link-up exist today, still trying to put victims of these procedures back in touch with their lost families, 20 or more years after these bodies were made defunct. These times are recorded for Australians and others, in books such as *If Everyone Cared* by Margaret Tucker, *My Place* by Sally Morgan, *Wandering Girl* by Glenyse Ward and *The Lost Children* by Coral Edwards and Peter Read.

But this was a 1950s society in which the policy of assimilation to the received Anglo-Australian model hardly needed articulating and had scarcely been questioned in the public forum, even by the many recently arrived post-war refugees and immigrants who might have been more immediately aware of the injustices and inequities it implied, although the effort required in re-establishing themselves in this new land would scarcely have left much energy to deal with these issues. These were the days when the national government was making the country freely available to the British to conduct nuclear testing – nuclear testing in Central Australia where indigenous peoples were still leading traditional lives. These were the days too, remembered clearly by older Australians, when England was considered *H*ome. While not necessarily an attitude general within the community, it was a fact that radio news programmes would announce 'And now the news from *H*ome . . .' (i.e. England). It was a fact, too, that without any great degree of difficulty, we accepted that 'the *Near* East' (the Middle East) and 'the *Far* East' (South-East Asia) were described by terms which were the exact reverse of our true geographical position. In an official sense, then, we looked out upon the world as if Australia really lay on the western edge of Europe. It all seems extraordinary today. We were brought up on images of Britain (which really meant England). My primary and secondary education took place during the 1950s and early 1960s, but it wasn't very different to that described so aptly by Shirley Hazzard (1980) in *The Transit of Venus*, even though about a period almost 20 years earlier:

> 'Grey Winter hath gone, like a wearisome guest,
> And, behold, for repayment,
> September comes in with the wind of the West
> And the Spring in her raiment.'

You might recite it in Elocution Class, but could hardly have it in English poetry. It was as if the poet had deliberately taken the losing, and Australian, side. He had grasped the nettle. But a nettle grasped remains a nettle, and grasping is an unnatural act. What was natural was hedgerows, hawthorn, skylarks, the chaffinch on the orchard bough. You had never seen these but believed in them with perfect faith. As you believed, also, in the damp, deciduous and rightful seasons of English literature and in lawns of emerald velours, or in flowers that could only be grown in Australia when the drought broke and with top-dressing. Literature had not simply made these things true. It had placed Australia in perpetual, flagrant violation of reality.

It is very difficult for healthy growth to take place when the mirror does not reflect what is there. If the image is indistinct or distorted, then surely a sense of dissatisfaction and discontent along with an unbalanced development must result. Educators with experience acknowledge the basic educational premise that learning proceeds from the known dimension, moving by degrees into the unknown. I was reminded by the Australian poet and teacher Dorothy Green (Auchterlonie) (*The National Times*, September 1979) that the most effective learning starts with the known, the familiar (in the Australian context, if you will, with the kookaburra), before building upon this secure basis and moving towards the unknown, the unfamiliar and, to complete the metaphor, the nightingale. Paolo Freire, that wise Brazilian educator who wrought miracles by practising the following simple yet profound principles, was another who confirmed for me that some of the tentative steps I was taking in working with Australian literature reflective of the experiences of my students were indeed moving in the right direction:

> ... educators have to work with the experiences that students, adults and other learners bring to schools and other educational sites. This means making those experiences in their public and private forms the object of debate and confirmation: it means legitimating such experiences in order to give those who move within them a sense of affirmation and to provide the conditions for students and others to display an active voice and presence. The pedagogical experience here becomes an invitation to make visible the language, dreams, values and encounters that constitute the lives of those whose histories are often actively silenced.
>
> (Freire, 1985: xxi–xxii)

There was very little literature that I studied at school which was Australian. But there were some pieces. In primary school, it was the humour of the nineteenth-century bush ballads that I remember, especially when Mr Shanahan, with obvious relish, roared the line from A.B. 'Banjo' Paterson's 'The Man from Ironbark' (about the mountain yokel on whom a city barber plays a practical joke with the blunt edge of his razor for the amusement of his waiting city clients): 'And "Murder! Bloody murder!" yelled the man from Ironbark.' This was especially enjoyable for the loud, public proclamation of the taboo word 'Bloody' as for anything else. I can't really recall any further Australian literature being studied until my final, matriculation year in secondary school in 1965. The question which arises out of this reflection has to do with what effects such a schizoid dissociation of the focus of learning from the physical and social reality must have for students. How do children ultimately cope when the milieu in which they live is challenged consciously and constantly by another and alien reality?

There are Australian writers such as Les A. Murray and Colin Thiele who admit that they wrote poems and stories specifically set within the Australian landscape because they had been fed a diet of other-world writing or because

they had heard people say that there was no such thing as Australian literature (nor ever could be, either). The writer Christopher Koch wrote in 1979
of a visit he made with poet Vivian Smith to the former penal settlement of
Maria Island on the East Coast of the state of Tasmania:

> It was the first time I had been across there, and both of us found the seascape
> around us strange and unfamiliar, although both of us were native Tasman-
> ians. The grey-green swell; the cold, stark light; the mournful deserted island
> with its ruined convict station; what did they remind us of?
>
> We imagined the scene to be like the Hebrides – although neither of us had
> been to Scotland. But we finally concluded that it probably resembled nowhere
> else: it was simply itself, and Tasmanian. We were victims, we realised, of a
> colonial habit of mind – always seeking other landscapes in our own. And
> Vivian said something then that I have often remembered: that a country and
> its landscapes perhaps don't fully exist until they have been written about –
> until poets and novelists create them.

In my final year of school, I studied Judith Wright's poem 'South of My
Days'. It was set in the New England region of New South Wales. It
specifically mentioned Tamworth, the city where I lived, and it referred to
other places in the locale which I knew and had visited, and there were
characters from the past including the local bushranger (outlaw) 'Thunder-
bolt'. The countryside it painted was immediately recognizable. It was local,
as indeed was the poet. And yet, in our classroom, there was no investigation
of the characters and places and events commemorated in the poem. And
there was no 'meeting' with the poet either. No, we engaged in a Leavisite
critical analysis of structure and language, ignoring the poet and the personal
connections we might have made from our experience. To say that 'we
engaged' in this literary critique is not quite correct either. We were handed
out printed material that contained the analysis which we, in turn, were to
learn and regurgitate for the ultimate examination. And yet there we had
been, so close, studying local literature at last. But this time it was a kind of
literary theory which thwarted a connection of literature with experience.

About 10 years ago, I drew a map of my childhood neighbourhood, start-
ling myself at the recall of faces and names and streetscape. I was responding
to a suggestion made at a seminar concerning ways in which we might
become more effective agents of change. One of the participants referred to
the self-revelatory process of asking oneself a series of questions leading
further and further backwards in time, retracing the steps taken and the
choices made, which had resulted ultimately in one's present professional
and philosophical pursuit.

And what had I found? In the 1950s and early 1960s, I grew up in a
comparatively large inland rural town. Although I was born in Sydney, as
were both my parents, a decision had been made in 1951 to move from this
metropolis. Despite the accidental death of my father pursuing this intention, my mother, aged 21, my baby brother and myself fulfilled the shared

dream of my parents and we found ourselves in Tamworth before the end of that year.

Like our first landlords, the Chinese/Anglo-Australian Yee family, we were members of the fundamental American-Protestant Seventh-day Adventist Church. Of the elderly Yee couple who had come from Guandong/ Hong Kong in 1900 – the year prior to Australia's Federation and the introduction of the Dictation Test, the term for what became otherwise known as the 'White Australia Policy', an exclusion policy which still dogs the national reputation despite having being abandoned in spirit for about 35 years and more than half that time in fact – I found Mrs Yee most fascinating, not so much for her limited English (even after more than 60 years in Australia) but for her tiny slippered feet upon which she hobbled to her pew each Sabbath. This was living history in fact, for she had been a victim of the cruel foot-binding custom not formally abolished in China until 1911. The local church to which we belonged was largely made up of people who had been converted from a variety of other faiths, although there were a number of families who could count several generations of their family as adherents. We were all 'different' from 'the world', both in our Sabbath observance (sunset Friday to sunset Saturday) and in our dietary laws (no pork or shellfish, smoking or alcohol, tea or coffee), and we were a strong missionary church, proselytizing and witnessing for our faith being absolutely integral to our membership. The missionary field for me was not only the place where I lived nor my country, but included a specific focus on the South Pacific. Members of my local church had relatives who were 'missionaries' (teachers, medical workers, pastors) in this vast field, and their slide shows and accompanying talks when they visited on their furloughs home captivated my attention. While my memory today suggests a patronizing colonial frame of reference to the medical missionary work, as well as a concentration on the exotic differences of those exciting cultures which were being 'tamed' from Satan's influences and 'civilized' by Western values as interpreted by this version of Christianity, it was, none the less, an important outward-looking focus for me during my adolescent years.

And in my neighbourhood, as revealed in my map, I encountered a wide variety of people, representative of the diverse backgrounds of the nation as a whole. There were two families from the Netherlands. The Goedhart family (later spelled Goodhart) from Den Helder eventually moved to Sydney following the completion of the nearby Keepit Dam Project. The Hoitinga family, from Sneek in Friesland, returned there, spent some time in Surinam, and then again went back to Sneek. In the late 1950s, it was rather unusual for anyone other than children to ride bicycles, but the father, a taciturn man who did, was, it was generally agreed in the neighbourhood, a communist. This was just a short distance in time from the Western world's paranoid witch-hunts. The USA had McCarthy; Australia had the Petrov Commission, though none of this meant anything to me at the time. Nor did this consensus of opinion affect our social intercourse with our neighbours. Another bike-riding neighbour, Pietro Bertoli, had about him too the taint of the communist connection. This irascible middle-aged immigrant from Italy was a bogey-man to the neighbourhood children while they were little, but it was another neighbour and immigrant, from England, who must have recognized the dreadful loneliness of this man and who consequently employed him as a gardener at both his home and at his nearby radio station, which added some measure of dignity and importance to his existence.

Ernest Higginbotham was the region's pioneer radio network developer. He later set up the first local TV station, which in the mid-1960s (well before the days of satellites as media transmitters) covered the second-largest area of any television station in the world. Or so we were told. (New World societies are very keen on these sorts of statistics, a type of cultural cringe to the Old World which I would like to believe is somewhat passé, although commercial interests nevertheless seem to encourage them.) This man was very important to me, not just because my mother worked for him one day a week as the house-cleaner, riding her bicycle to work (she wasn't a communist, but then *she* was *born* in Australia!), but more because we shared birthdays and 29 May meant treasured letters (still in my possession) and gifts (especially of United Nations stamps) and an abiding interest in my educational progress.

And among my other neighbours, including retired farmers, public servants, schoolteachers, builders and trades-people came a young Koori couple. This was not long before I left Tamworth to pursue my tertiary studies at Sydney University. While I cannot be certain, I suspect that their presence was a part of the new government policy of integration. Its implementation at our local community level meant that Koori people were to be moved from their settlement (a collection of shacks put together out of discarded building materials) near the municipal dump and dispersed away from each other throughout the town. The historical fact that like people often congregate together in a more or less fluid reality was not recognized nor understood in those days. Their name was Munro (surely a connection with Billy), and when I came home from university during vacations it was to find that my little half-sister's playmate was their daughter Lisa-Jane.

When I was growing up, clearly we saw the differences which surrounded us – and heard and smelled them as well. But, except perhaps in private, they were differences which I don't generally recollect as being commented upon. When we fought among ourselves as children, it seemed that our parents united in one front to punish us for our silliness, and not being allowed to play together quickly allied us all in a resolve to get together again. And when people moved away we stayed in touch. But apart from this, the differences which existed were not especially celebrated and nor were they necessarily seen as having a positive dimension. My stepfather certainly saw very little of worth in anything which didn't conform. Thus it was only years later, when I drew up my map, after I had travelled and lived abroad and returned to an Australia which was shaking off many of its past inequities, that I was able to look back and see just how rich had been my growing-up place, and to set it all in some sort of perspective.

As for my own immediate family, I trace descent out of East Anglia (paternal great-great-great-grandparents arriving in the First Fleet on 26 January 1788), Cambridgeshire, the West Riding of Yorkshire, Kent (maternal grandfather), Dumfries and Roxburghshire (paternal grandmother) in the UK. One aunt married a Canadian and lived out her life as a Mormon in the USA, another married a German immigrant and spent a great deal of her married life in Malaysia, and a third saw a daughter marry a French man and go to live in France. My brother married a French woman whom he met in Eire and they live in Tamworth, NSW. An uncle married a Chinese woman who came originally from the island of Bangka in Indonesia, but who had spent many years living in Germany. My maternal great-grandfather was born in Fiji in 1876 (of mixed Sussex and German parents) and a first cousin married a Canadian and lives in Canada. An examination of my Kable Family Tree as prepared in 1983 reveals names of French, German, Greek, Irish, Maltese, Polish, Russian, Scottish and other origins. My wife's father arrived as a teenager in Australia from Northumberland just before the Great Depression. His father had spent some time in South Africa seeking diamonds without success. Australia as a nation is both diverse and new. Of the current population of 17 million, one in five was born overseas, while another one in five has at least one parent born overseas. The picture I have presented of my family background is not at all untypical of most Australians.

During the time I was studying at Sydney University, I discovered quite a lot more about my world. There was Peta Terry, who arrived in 1960 from Harbin in China and whose Latin teacher in Sydney in 1962 was my Latin teacher in Tamworth in 1963, Mrs Henson, who with her husband had left South Africa following the 1961 Sharpeville Massacre. Robyn Chan was the daughter of Harry Chan, Mayor of Darwin and the first Australian of Chinese background to hold such an office anywhere in Australia. My neighbours were Greek and Italian and I boarded in one household with Stewart Cheng who was an overseas student from Hong Kong. I used to test my landlady on her Italian over breakfast and discovered her connections with the literary left of Australia in the early part of this century only many years later, when it finally meant something to me.

All of this background was good preparation for my teaching practice year, during which I spent periods in both elementary and secondary schools noted for their numbers of students of non-English-speaking backgrounds. I began with a fortnight at Paddington Primary School. This was one of the pioneer schools in Australia in teaching English as a second language. I observed a kindergarten class in which not one child spoke English and yet most had been born in Australia. This was a revelation to me. I taught a year

6 class in the same school in which many of the students were from Spain. At J.J. Cahill Memorial High School, my students were from a whole variety of backgrounds, including Greek, Serbian, Russian and Italian. It was a challenging yet exhilarating year.

I had a lot of lessons to learn in my early years of teaching. There were directions already being taken and sentiments of attachment to the underdog which I already held that, looking back now, I can see were leading me to the moment when I would begin to tackle the major issues of prejudice and bigotry, discrimination and racism. And of course the issue was not just the underdog, the children and adults in our society who were the targets of racism; there was also the humbug of educational practice which had to be recognized and cast aside in order to permit real learning to take place.

Some aspects of the humbug which I learnt early to dispel included the distance I was supposed to keep between myself and my students. In the small rural town of Hay, where I commenced teaching, this would have been impossible anyway, but the 'advice' proffered by my Principal concerning the low social standing of particular families who were henceforth to be avoided was not at all appreciated. I was also able to prove in practice the fallacy of IQ and of standardized testing in general as a predictor of success, demonstrating to myself the efficacy of positive teacher expectations and encouragement. (Only later did I learn about the hidden cultural assumptions underlying such testing procedures, which made them even more abhorrent to me.) I began to learn, too, the connection between a well-prepared lesson delivered with enthusiasm and the presence of humour, and the gradual disappearance of classroom management difficulties. I learnt above all to like young people and to enjoy my profession.

Interspersed as they were with discovering the physical beauty of south-eastern Australia, as well as journeys overseas which brought my national identity into some sort of focus, there are a number of instances connected with the first few years of my teaching which remain clearly inscribed in my memory. One was the astonishment of a 14-year-old girl called Jutta that I was able to write her name correctly and without comment as I compiled the class roll, the first time this had happened with a new teacher in her 9 years at school. And I taught Koori students for the first time. I realize now that the curriculum contained no honest reflection of their cultural presence and was effectively a gate locked against their entry. The resistance I was to encounter from some of these students was their unconscious response. But one student, Gayle Kennedy, cousin to Evonne Goolagong, Wimbledon tennis champion, revealed a gift for writing. Gayle became the recipient of a scholarship to Queenwood Girls' School in Sydney where she completed her final 2 years of secondary schooling. We corresponded for a while. Even then, with the little I understood of Koori Australia, it appeared she was destined for an important life. At our last meeting about 7 years ago, she was preparing to make a film on the Koori people of western New South Wales.

In 1974, newly married, my wife and I were appointed to a new high school in the north of the state, not far from the Queensland border. My developing awareness of prejudice and its racist manifestation was to be sharpened in this town. For the first time, I clearly remember seeing that racism wasn't something confined elsewhere, especially to South Africa or the southern states of the USA, to which our self-righteous indignation was often directed. It was present in my own community and yet I had not been able to see it clearly before, particularly in relation to Koori Australians. It had only been 7 years previously that a national referendum, by a clear majority of 90 per cent of the population, had given responsibility for Kooris to the federal government and finally accorded them citizenship. (Dr Eve Fesl of the Koori Research Centre, Monash University, believes that true equality before the law in terms of citizenship did not actually exist until 1984. In that year, as for all other Australians, voting was made compulsory for Koori Australians. What this meant was that they could now call on the law to protect them against the harrassment suffered by many rural Koori communities in attempts to dissuade them from enfranchising themselves.) However, by 1974, the first Land Rights were about to be granted by the Whitlam-led Federal Parliament, which was also cutting our overt colonial presence by granting independence to Papua New Guinea. The winds of social change were blowing so noisily that it was difficult to remain unaware. And on top of this was a new Minister for Immigration, who was talking of the concept of multiculturalism, a term borrowed from Canada and adapted to the local scene. This was a giant step forward from the old assimilationist and integrationist policies. Cultural pluralism and diversity of backgrounds were being highlighted as positive elements of the Australian national character. But in this highlighting many inequalities were being exposed. And so external factors as well as personal experiences were raising my level of consciousness.

There was a significant number of Koori students in our new high school. Most came from the little village of Tingha and most were victims of the institutionally discriminatory practice of streaming (placement in graded classes on the basis of standardized testing procedures). Overnight excursions taken by my wife and myself uncovered personalities of great intelligence and wit among these Koori students which were never sighted at school. And although I was still woefully ignorant of Koori cultures, I recall earnest defences of Koori students as I rose to the bait of racist asides at social gatherings. The spectre of Billy Munro and of my little sister's playmate, and Gayle Kennedy too, stood beside me and gave me the courage to disagree with my friends. I witnessed some of the ways in which Koori people were slighted in the town. On one occasion I was left in a shaking, voiceless fury, and it was this feeling of helplessness which led me to my first attempt to treat the issue in the classroom.

My students were aged around 15 and I knew that most of them would leave school at the end of the year. I hadn't really properly defined the issues of prejudice and bigotry to myself, apart from a recognition of injustice based on an apparent difference. But one of the students in my class, Athol Boney, was Koori, and both for him and his classmates I felt a pressing need to attempt some redress of general community assumptions, no matter how difficult I found this programme. Out of my dilemma I sought the voices of others who had addressed these concerns in literature. They would be able to articulate my disquiet far more eloquently. In the process, I also exposed another educational myth, the one which suggests that 'story' is *not* the most important thing to take from literature. 'I dips me lid' (as poet C.J. Dennis put 'I take my hat off') to those educators who had selected various pieces of literature for study in our schools of the calibre present on the shelves of our textbook room. I wasn't yet looking for Australian writing, although there were some classic examples already in existence (and which I discovered later), but we did have Alan Paton's *Cry, the Beloved Country* and Harper Lee's *To Kill A Mockingbird*, both powerful novels which arouse a sense of outrage at the human injustices they unfold. And yet, both societies were clearly distinct from our own, and it was the local connection which was the most important and the hardest to make. In fact, it was the brilliant poem 'Telephone Conversation', by the Nigerian writer (and 1986 recipient of the Nobel Prize for Literature) Wole Soyinka, which came closest. Those ties to England, in which Wole Soyinka's poem was set, describing the frustrating attempts of an African student to secure accommodation, were still not very loose at this time. My valid passport of the time, issued in 1971, proclaimed that I was both an Australian citizen *and* a British subject.

The impact that unit of work may have had subsequently in the lives of my students I will probably never know, for it was just shortly afterwards that my wife and I left that place, setting out on our own great adventure. It was during this journey of 18 months that we passed through three continents and spent most of the time living in non-English-speaking countries, learning valuable lessons about powerlessness and cultural differences and, as the ultimate shock, finding England quite incomprehensible on many levels and not the 'Home' I'd been conditioned for so long to expect.

Back in Australia in 1978, without permanent employment, I tackled some gherkin packing on a farm at Eurunderee, just outside Mudgee in the central west of New South Wales. This was next door to the place where Henry Lawson, one of the nation's greatest writers of the late nineteenth and early twentieth centuries, grew up, a landscape where he set many of his stories. For the first time, I felt a sense of Australia's history and of Australian writing. My time outside Australia now operated as a microscope through which I saw all sorts of aspects of my country and society up close, sharply defined by those differences experienced overseas. In the following year, my wife and I moved to Sydney where I was able to make use of my experience teaching English as a Foreign Language in Madrid and Munich by teaching English to immigrants and refugees to Australia. Once I had some of the strategies involved in this process under control, and had commenced various studies into the linguistic and societal aspects of the profession in which I was now engaged, I began to feel able to begin a critical appraisal of it. And it was while teaching adults at a New Arrivals Hostel Education Centre that my frustration at the lack of Australian-based resources and at the overreliance on British materials prepared for a holidaying or business language market in middle-class Europe became most pointed. My learners weren't interested in airport timetables, travelling on the Underground or booking rooms in London hotels. But they did want to know about Australia, about its history and its people and its idiom. It was just before I returned to an appointment in the secondary school system that I began exploring some of these features with my classes.

It was a turning point, of course, and one which was highlighted by discovering exactly the same sorts of resources available to me at Homebush Boys' High School, where I had been appointed a teacher of English-as-a-Second Language (ESL), as I had been discarding at the adult education centre. Apart from finding myself having to do battle on a fairly grand scale against such blights on education as corporal punishment and streaming, particularly as they affected immigrant and refugee students within their first 2 years in Australia, I found myself answering the broader curriculum and syllabus objectives which my students had to meet at both junior and senior levels. The response from my students, pleased to be treated as equals with their English-speaking peers and using the same texts as they were, was highly encouraging. I was abandoning the structured and simplified or bowdlerized readers of which they had a surfeit. The distortion of the normal rhythm and stress of written English and the excision of the usual language redundancies and other richness of usage made them anathema. Later I became aware that these same 'books', filling many ESL bookshelves, had originally been designed for those labelled 'slow learners', back in the days when deficit theories held sway. The equation was quite clear: a second language learner was a slow learner was a second language learner.

Colin Thiele's *The Sun on the Stubble* is a story set in rural South Australia, peopled with characters whose German origins are drawn as much by their patterns of speech as by names and cultural celebrations. As I read the story aloud to my class of year 8 boys, all of whom were from South-East Asia (Burma, Hong Kong, Laos, Taiwan, Vietnam), I began to dredge my own memory for stories with which to illustrate the gaps between the story's setting and my students' own life experiences. My genuine childhood fears of falling into the deep pit toilet of a house in which we lived while my widowed mother spent a year caring for an Alzheimer-affected retired farmer in a small village just outside Tamworth provoked a variety of toilet 'stories' from my students. This was the first time in which I had used literature in such a way to draw out this kind of connection. My students demonstrated something of the liberating power of literature which explains life. Later the same year, when Colin Thiele won Children's Book of the Year with *The Valley Between*, my students who had claimed him as their writer felt more than justified in their enjoyment of a book which not only told them about Australia, but which also offered images of fellow newcomers to this place. The highest accolade was when one of these students, less than 2 years in Australia, went out and bought one of Colin Thiele's books for himself.

For a senior class of year 11 students, I selected the *The Mango Tree*, a novel by Ronald McKie which traces a young boy's journey to maturity. With a small rural Queensland town as his setting, the author presents images of a culturally diverse Australia back in the days surrounding the Great War: the German farmers and the Chinatown inhabitants, both befriended by young Jamie's grandmother; the remittance man from England (kept here by regular sums remitted by family) known as the Professor, who reminds Jamie of the presence of the original Koori people of that district; the Italian musicians; the Greek-born Georgi Comino; the Gaelic-speaking Bandy Mac; and the three principal churches facing each other in the town and reflecting other cultural perspectives – 'The Catholic Church with its white virgin outside, the Church of England with its green spire and leadlight windows, the Presbyterian Church of plain God-fearing board, and all in a group lowering suspiciously at one another like family enemies at a wake.' As we read the book together, the richness of language which was initially rather daunting to the students, and the images of Australia which it articulated, became the very features which gripped their interest. Again, as with my junior class, I found myself not so much explaining the meanings of words as telling stories which added depth to McKie's cultural allusions. A letter from the author in the *Sydney Morning Herald* caught my attention and I wrote him a very self-conscious letter (my first to a writer) explaining our study and enjoyment of his book. Several months later a reply arrived. He'd been in England undertaking research. He generously invited questions from the students. After some prompting, they tackled this genuine task, their first letters in English. Their writing clearly demonstrated to Ronald McKie their various levels of structural fluency, but it was the voices from the heart which shone through most strongly. He responded magnificently, referring to his many years in South-East Asia to the delight of the majority of the class. Several took up the invitation to visit. For these students, the novel took on an entirely different dimension as a result of this connection. This was 'their' book. And the sense of being special in the study of this book will no doubt linger in their memories forever. Their next book was the journalistic diary of a young Australian woman called Frances Letters, who wrote of her experiences when travelling in South-East Asia over a decade before, *The Surprising Asians*. I did not need to motivate or persuade, cajole or in any other way promote this book. It was about their countries as seen through the eyes of an Australian. The subject matter was the motivation. I had stumbled upon another secret.

Suddenly, I was seeing Australia anew, through the eyes and experiences of those who were recently arrived here, and then further illuminated by some close literary observations. I sought for more images in writing which drew upon this immigrant experience. One of the founders in the 1930s of the Jindyworobak Movement, a rejection of European forms and themes in favour of a literary connection to the Australian landscape, was Rex Ingamells. He wrote an epic poem, *The Great South Land*. A fragment titled 'Cheng Ho' was in a school anthology I used with my year 10 class. Greeted with cries of recognition by more students from Chinese backgrounds, Cheng Ho, I learnt, was a very famous admiral in Chinese history. At the beginning of the fifteenth century, he had sailed as far as the east coast of Africa. Rex Ingamells was suggesting the not unlikely proposition that he may have even touched on the northern coast of Australia. This was quite astounding for me, brought up on an Anglo-centric view of Australian history. A later reading of the epic itself showed that an important early seventeenth-century Japanese trader, Yamada Nagamasa, may also have sailed down the east coast of Australia, 150 years before James Cook. But for my Chinese students, the literary references to one of their historical heroes linking him to Australia was quite exciting. This encouraged me to discuss with them the very real possibility mentioned to me by a friend who had spent time in China that the expression 'dinkum' (as in the essential Australian idiomatic expression, 'fair dinkum', meaning true, reliable, genuine, honest) was in fact from the Chinese 'din-kum', meaning 'real gold'. Several others with a specific interest in the connections between China and Australia such as Eric Rolls (literary articulator of our history) and Morag Loh (oral historian) have confirmed this speculation.[2] At any rate, my students were happy to consider this Chinese contribution to the most Australian of expressions. I had not long read both books of American writer Maxine Hong Kingston (*Warrior Woman, China Men*), in which she revealed the hitherto largely ignored and hidden Chinese participation in the history of the USA. The same elements were a factor of the way in which Australians, too, saw their own history. And when I read the chapter from *Warrior Woman* about 'Lo Bun Son', my Chinese students recognized him immediately.

Rex Ingamells also led me to reflections of Koori Australia, but this was a shadowy spotlight whose focus was later sharpened by the writing of Koori poet Oodgeroo Noonuccal (then still known as Kath Walker). The realization that the best voices for presenting particular cultural experiences belonged to those who had lived them was beginning to make itself clear to me. Peter Skrzynecki was one writer whose poetry was measured against the lives of my students, deepening their own sense of awareness. We felt we could trust these writers, even if there were differences between our various experiences and those they described. But we also found some pieces which demonstrated racist writing quite clearly. The dictionaries came in handy as we did our best to find a connection between words such as 'bucks' and 'paws' and human beings. We didn't find the connection. But we did discover one way of testing veracity in the written word. We wanted to believe that the author herself, an expatriate Australian, might shudder today at her cultural assumptions and choice of language, as we reminded ourselves about trying to put a piece of writing into the historical perspective of the time in which it was written. But then again, perhaps it has always been the mark of a true writer to not only see the differences between peoples but beyond them as well to the universal dignity and integrity of all cultures.

Since that time, I have held a variety of positions. They have given me the time to think, and research and test my ideas on Australian writing. I have been involved in teaching adult classes of specific cultural and linguistic backgrounds or of the more usual groups which randomly come together from a variety of linguistic backgrounds to pursue a study of English. I have used short pieces of Australian writing as a focus not just on our cultural diversity and history and experiences but as a mirror which reflects the individual reality of us all. And I have returned to the secondary English classroom, teaching English to native speakers. My continued interest in action research, observing and writing about the responses of my students over the past 5 years, tells me that all young people want to be able to read and discuss and write reflectively on the central issue of our varying cultural identities in this land. They want to be able to feel pride in their own ethnic origins as well as to examine the inequities of our society, in its history as well as in its contemporary concerns. They have social consciences which feel for the downtrodden and they want to be able to take a stand on the deeper moral values of our times. Literature allows this to happen. And in the reflection it offers on our national life and in the gasp of recognition with which such examination is inevitably greeted, comes the chance to leap off into a richer and more secure life.

At the beginning of 1986, at Writers' Week in Sydney, Sneja Gunew suggested that it was the cultural perspective which would become the key issue for judging the honesty of literature from that point onwards. I agree. It *has* to be central to our judgement in a world where we are increasingly acknowledging our cultural diversity. Within the Australian setting, there is a considerable and growing body of literature which tells Australians about themselves and their environment. This telling is best when it folds itself around the truths of our fundamental cultural features. These features are the ones which unite us as human beings, while at the same time outlining those marvellously rich and varied differences passed on from our diverse ethnic origins.

Notes

1 Koori is a word from the New South Wales central coast indigenous peoples meaning 'person', and is increasingly replacing the Latin-based terms Aborigine/ Aboriginal (with their accretions of negative connotations in the Australian context), especially in the South-eastern part of the country, as the term for the indigenous peoples of Australia. Elsewhere within Australia, terms such as 'Murri', 'Nyoongah' and 'Nungah' are used for the same reason.

2 Apparently, in a Sze Yap dialect from Guandong Province, from where came most nineteenth-century Chinese to Australia, 'din-kum' means 'real gold'. A minor skirmish in a column of the *Sydney Morning Herald* tried to pour scorn on the idea, but in 1988 my initial comment was listed in the *Australian National Dictionary* under the word *dinkum*. And this is fair dinkum!

References

Bostock, G. and Morgan, A. (Producers) (1983). *Lousy Little Sixpence* (film). Sydney, NSW: Sixpence Productions.

Davis, J. (1978). *Jagardoo*. North Ryde, NSW: Methuen Australia.

Dennis, C.J. (1915). *The Sentimental Bloke*. North Ryde, NSW: Angus and Robertson.

Edwards, C. and Read, P. (1987). *The Lost Children*. Australia: Doubleday.

Franklin, M. (1901). *My Brilliant Career*. North Ryde, NSW: Angus and Robertson.

Freire, P. (1985). *The Politics of Education (Culture, Power and Liberation)*. Bergin and Garvey.

Green, D. (1979). Puzzling lack of passion for our own literature. *The National Times*, 20 October, pp. 35–6.

Gunew, S. (ed.) (1982). *Displacements*. Geelong, Vic.: Deakin University Press.

Gunew, S. (ed.) (1987). *Displacements 2*. Geelong, Vic.: Deakin University Press.

Hazzard, S. (1980). *The Transit of Venus*. New York: Viking.

Ingamells, R. (1951). *The Great South Land*. Melbourne, Vic.: Georgian House.

Kable, J. (1984). The deep end of the schoolyard. In *Topics in ESL*, No. 4. Sydney, NSW: Department of Education, Multicultural Education Centre, NSW.

Kingston, M.H. (1976). *Woman Warrior*. London: Picador.

Kingston, M.H. (1981). *China Men*. London: Picador.

Koch, C. (1987). Maria Island visit. In Pierce, P. (ed.), *The Oxford Literary Guide to Australia*. Melbourne: Oxford University Press.

Lawson, H. (1959). *Fifteen Stories*. North Ryde, NSW: Angus and Robertson.

Lee, H. (1960). *To Kill a Mockingbird*. London: Heinemann.

Letters, F. (1968). *The Surprising Asians*. Sydney, NSW: Angus and Robertson.

McKie, R. (1974). *The Mango Tree*. London: Collins.

Morgan, S. (1987). *My Place*. Fremantle, WA: Fremantle Arts Centre Press.

Murray, E.K.M. (1977). *Caught in the Web of Words*. New York: Yale University Press.

Murray, L.A. (1982). *The Vernacular Republic*. North Ryde, NSW: Angus and Robertson.

Noonuccal, O. (1981). *My People*, 2nd edn. Molton, Qd: Jacaranda.

Paterson, A.B. 'Banjo' (1946). *Collected Verse*. North Ryde, NSW: Angus and Robertson.

Paton, A. (1948). *Cry, the Beloved Country*. London: Jonathan Cape.

Richardson, H.H. (1930). *The Fortunes of Richard Mahony*. London: Heinemann.

Simon, E. (1978). *Through My Eyes*. Sydney, NSW: William Collins.

Soyinka, W. (1975). Telephone Call. In Foster, J.L. (ed.), *Black and White*. Oxford: Pergamon Press.

Thiele, C. (1973). *The Sun on the Stubble*. Kent Town, SA: Rigby.

Thiele, C. (1981). *The Valley Between*. Kent Town, SA: Rigby.

Tucker, M. (1977). *If Everyone Cared*. Sydney, NSW: Ure Smith.

Ward, G. (1987). *Wandering Girl*. Perth: W.A. Magabala Books.

White, P. (1955). *The Tree of Man*. Harmondsworth: Penguin.

Wright, J. (1975). South of my Days. In *Collected Poems*. Sydney, NSW: Angus and Robertson.

PART TWO
Case studies

5 'Journey to Jo'burg': Reading a novel with years 7 and 8

SHAHANA MIRZA

Introduction

The following case study demonstrates one way in which students can be introduced to multicultural and anti-racist issues through the study of a piece of literature. The study resulted from work done with two classes at Chessington Community College. Chessington is a newly formed community college in the Borough of Kingston upon Thames. Kingston has a grammar/ secondary modern school system, and therefore the college has an intake of students who have not entered grammar school.

One of the classes involved in the project consisted of 27 year 7 students. The class was of mixed ability and the students were in the main white, with one student being from mixed race. The second class consisted of 24 students in year 8; once again, this was a mixed-ability group with only one black student. The text studied was *Journey to Jo'burg*, by Beverley Naidoo. It outlines the story of two black South African children who travel to Johannesburg to find their mother. The story highlights the difficulties that black people face because of the apartheid laws.

Preparatory work

The lesson began by finding out how much students already knew about the situation in South Africa. Both classes brainstormed the words 'South Africa'. It became apparent that there was a vast range of knowledge and ability. In both classes, the students considered Africa to be a land of famine, wildlife or jungle. Many were unable to differentiate between South Africa and the rest of the continent. Only a small proportion of students considered the words apartheid and racism in their discussions. Two students knew who President De Klerk was. During the discussion that followed, it became evident that the majority of students had only vague ideas about South Africa, much of which had come from the media or from relatives who had visited the country.

The first step was to read the book *Journey to Jo'burg*. The preface provides the reader with two newspaper articles with commentary, which immediately give the story a political stance. The articles are introduced by a rather bold, emotive statement: '. . . for this is the land of apartheid where the broken families are all black. The people who make the laws are all white.' Many of the students took the statement literally. In later project work, they wanted to launch campaigns to 'help the poor black people'. This condescending attitude seemed to rise directly from the introductory statements in the book and not from the story of *Journey to Jo'burg*. Some of these issues will be discussed later.

The newspaper articles at the beginning of the book were about children who had travelled hundreds of kilometres to see their parents who had been forced to work in faraway towns. They gave the book a realistic setting. As these events had happened only recently, they also gave the story a sense of immediacy. Before reading the story, the students discussed the setting and tried to locate South Africa on a world map. Thus, they began to have a clearer idea about the background to the story and the place in which it was set.

Reading the book

In addition to studying the basic themes, story and characterization in the text, the students were encouraged to consider the issues of apartheid and racism. They read the first three chapters, at which point there was a break for discussion. The aim was to clarify the role of the main characters in the story. Each group selected a different character and presented a short profile to the rest of the class.

Many of the students had difficulty pronouncing the names of characters. The year 8 students therefore decided to pronounce them phonetically. It was interesting to note that some of the first-year students were embarrassed and amused by some of the names. Through further discussion about names from different countries, we were able to overcome this. Thus the students became more sensitive to the importance of pronouncing names correctly.

After completion of chapters four to six, a second activity was introduced. The students were asked to 'hotseat' a character in the story, a technique whereby a volunteer pretends to be one of the characters and the group asks them questions about their thoughts, feelings and situation. One or two of the students were very articulate, drawing upon the information they had read to develop the characters further. The students playing the children became quite involved in the role play, expressing anger and despair at the fact that they were separated from their mother. The determination to rise above the 'oppression' was evident. The hotseating enabled the students to empathize with the characters in the story. They were very keen to read the next chapter, as they had begun to feel that the events described were really happening!

After reading chapters seven to ten, there were group discussions on the issues raised (e.g. the pass system in South Africa). Having been asked to write a short piece imagining they had been caught without a pass, students wrote of fear, anger, frustration and outrage. Some of them wrote from the viewpoint of the policeman arresting a black person for not having a pass: 'I'm just doing my job. I don't hate blacks, but I have to do as I'm told.' Many of the students were beginning to have a clearer idea of what it might be like to live as a black person in South Africa.

Having completed the book, each pupil wrote an individual evaluation of the text. They described what they had enjoyed about the book and considered what they had learnt – only 2 of 50 students stated that they did not enjoy reading *Journey to Jo'burg*, one of whom felt that the beginning was good but 'then it went downhill'. The remaining students seemed to have become very involved in the story:

> Usually I can never get into a book but . . . I felt I was one of them and that's why I enjoyed it.

> It was interesting and exciting.

> I enjoyed the adventure parts and when the fights happened.

Several students said they liked the book because it was 'easy to read'. This was particularly interesting, as prior to the project there had been some concern that as a piece of literature the text was not demanding enough. However, many of the poorer readers were able to follow the text easily. In both classes, the students were keen to read the story aloud as they were confident of being able to pronounce the words. Both classes became involved in the story and were keen to respond to the ideas put forward.

The students were asked to evaluate what they had learnt while reading the story. They were very clear about what they had achieved:

> I learnt about the pass system in South Africa.

> . . . how white people treat black people in South Africa . . .

> I learnt about racism and that white people don't give black people opportunities.

Further activities

In order to encourage further discussion of apartheid and South Africa, a number of students participated in further activities. They were given a selection of photographs portraying scenes in South Africa, e.g. a demonstration, a man being arrested by the police, a crowded bus. In pairs, having chosen a photograph to discuss in detail, they were to imagine that they were one of the people in the photograph and to describe their thoughts and feelings. Many vivid descriptions resulted. The students showed that they were able to imagine what South African people are experiencing: 'I am sick of being pushed around by white people' one student wrote, 'It is stupid'. One student imagined she was a child waiting in a hospital queue: 'I am lying in my mother's arms. I can't bear my mother holding me because it hurts. I can hear babies crying'.

Although some of the students portrayed black people as victims, many began to see more subtle issues. They described strong black people who were prepared to fight for their freedom. One student took the role of a white policeman and explained that he did not necessarily hate blacks: 'I'm just doing my job. If I don't I can't feed my family.' It was felt that this was not simply a black and white issue; the students had begun to consider the 'grey' areas.

Now that they were building up ideas about students in South Africa, they were provided with factual information about how apartheid came into existence and were given activities to help them consider some of the issues.

Background on South Africa (see Appendix 1, p. 89)

The students were provided with information about the history of apartheid. They discussed the following issues:

- How Dutch settlers drove out the natives of South Africa and forced them into slavery.
- Nelson Mandela's imprisonment: the students shared ideas they had picked up from the media and compared them to the text.
- The present situation: the students discussed how apartheid was being dismantled. Interest in South Africa had obviously been heightened and they were able to build upon the knowledge they already had and respond to questions about apartheid and sanctions.

Case study on Tozama Mafeke and Patty Brown (see Appendix 2, pp. 90–92)

The students were given information about two South African women. The first, Tozama Mafeke, was a black widow with a baby and two school age children; the second was a white mother of two children. The students were then asked to balance the budgets of the two women: Tozama on £40 a month and Patty on £1800. They had to take into account education, food, fuel, health, etc. Some of the students became very involved in trying to balance Tozama's budget, and found themselves having to decide between food and clothes or education, and whether or not they could afford to send a letter to a relative. Many of the students became frustrated when they were unable to make ends meet and they were thus able to empathize with black South Africans in general.

In contrast, those students who discussed Patty Brown's budget were able to buy all the necessities with plenty to spare for luxuries. They were able to see clearly the inequalities in South Africa, but as 'white South Africans' were not sure what course of action to take.

Information game (see Appendix 3, p. 93)

Each group of students was provided with an information sheet containing extracts from South African newspapers and other factual information. The aim was to use the information to create a short radio or TV bulletin. This enabled the students to see how facts can be manipulated in order to put across a different story. They also discussed censorship and considered how it might affect the news reports.

Project work

The students were given the opportunity to further develop their ideas through project work. Each group chose an issue to study in detail and their ideas were shared through group presentations. The topics ranged from apartheid and education to the climate in South Africa. It was particularly exciting to see the students using current news items, photographs and encyclopaedias to research their projects.

The results were interesting. Many of the students showed a heightened sensitivity to the situation of black South Africans and carefully presented factual information about their situation. Some of the students had the feeling that black people were victims and needed our help. They wanted to launch a campaign in order to raise money. Although this showed concern and enthusiasm, the discussion needed to go further. It was important to point out that black South Africans needed support and not pity – pity would only undermine black people and imply that they were incapable of helping themselves.

Finally, the classes pooled their ideas to produce work on South Africa that was displayed for the rest of the school to see.

Conclusion

The story of *Journey to Jo'burg* raised a number of important issues. It was evident that the students had been able to empathize with the main characters in the book; for example Naledi, who is portrayed as a determined, young black woman who, having decided what she wants, is able to achieve it. The students were able to understand the language of the text and therefore they were able to concentrate on the complex issues that it dealt with. The students were asked to evaluate what they had learnt, and the following are some of their responses:

> I learnt a lot about racism and life in South Africa. I thought it was disgusting the way black people were being treated in their own country.

I learnt about how different life could be just because of the colour of your skin. They story definitely got the message through.

I learnt that children went to school to learn to be servants, not for education . . .

The students' perceptions of the country had certainly developed a great deal. It was no longer a country where there was just famine and wildlife; it was a place where real people existed and where there was widespread inequality. Towards the end of the project it was announced that President De Klerk was taking steps to dismantle apartheid and the students avidly watched the news reports. One student wrote: 'I learnt that it is not easy for black people but because they are brave, the country is changing.'

References

Leeds Development Education Centre: South Africa Pack.

Macdonald, F. (1987). *Working for Equality*. London: Macdonald.

Naidoo, B. (1988). *Journey to Jo'burg: A South African Story*. London: Longman.

Appendix 1   Anti-apartheid

A divided land

It was after midnight on 16 May 1977. All night, Winnie Mandela had heard strange noises outside the house, but thought nothing of it. She was too busy working on her sociology project. The police were always patrolling the streets of Soweto, the black township outside Johannesburg where she and her daughter lived. All of a sudden, there was a tremendous noise outside, as if a hail of stones or bullets had landed on the roof. Then fists hammered on all the doors, walls and windows, and dogs bayed at the door. Outside, the yard was full of armed men.

'Come out!' they ordered. 'You're under arrest!'

Why did the South African authorities arrest Winnie Mandela? In order to answer this question, we need to look back into the history of southern Africa. The original inhabitants of the southernmost part of Africa were the Khoikhoi people. Over a thousand years ago, other black peoples, including the Zulus and the Xhosas, also moved into the region from the north. The lands were fertile and their crops and livestock prospered. The peoples who lived near the coast traded with Portuguese merchants who sailed to the Cape. News of this 'fine and generous' land soon spread to Europe, and in 1652 a group of Dutch farmers arrived, determined to settle. They soon drove the Khoikhoi people from their lands, and turned some of them into slaves. Gradually, the Dutch settlers, or 'Boers' as they called themselves, took over more and more land. And as they moved northward, they clashed with the Zulu and Xhosa peoples. The Boers believed that they had a God-given right to live in Africa, and to use the black Africans as their slaves. Not surprisingly, the black Africans fought back. The British also tried to seize a share of the land, partly to settle there but also because they wanted to mine for gold and diamonds. In the 19th century, Africa became a battlefield as the different groups fought for control of the land. In 1910, under British guidance, the former Dutch colonies were granted independence, and became the Dominion of South Africa. The effect of this was disastrous for everyone except the Boers and the British settlers.

In 1913 an act was passed which granted 88% of the land to the Boers and the British. The rest of the land was poor and would not support the black African people, and so they were forced to work for the white settlers. Wages were low and living conditions were often appalling. Except for the inhabitants of Cape Province, black people could not vote, and had no say in the country's affairs.

In the years that followed, conditions for the black Africans became even worse, as the political system known as apartheid (apart-ness) was developed. Winnie Mandela, her husband Nelson, and many other black people joined the African National Congress and fought against apartheid. They wanted equal rights for all people in South Africa. To the government, this was like fighting against the country itself. That is why they arrested Winnie Mandela and thousands like her.

> Nelson Mandela trained as a lawyer, and, before his trial, worked to help black people in need of legal advice.

In 1977, Winnie Mandela was exiled to the small white town of Brandfort. The South African government hoped that this would make it difficult for her to continue her campaign against apartheid.

The scramble for Africa! This map shows the areas originally occupied by African peoples, and the expansion of European settlement during the 18th and 19th centuries.

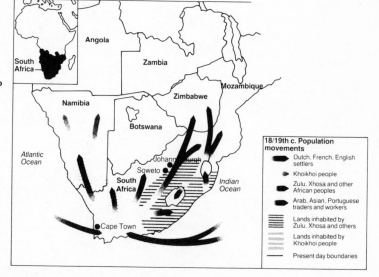

18/19th c. Population movements

- Dutch, French, English settlers
- Khoikhoi people
- Zulu, Xhosa and other African peoples
- Arab, Asian, Portuguese traders and workers
- Lands inhabited by Zulu, Xhosa and others
- Lands inhabited by Khoikhoi people
- Present day boundaries

Appendix 2

Question sheet

1 Do you think the family is able to have an adequate diet? How often do you think the family is able to eat eggs, meat, fish, milk or cheese? Or drink coke or wine? Or have a bar of chocolate? How often might they have a meal or snack out? Or have a dinner party?

2 How often can the woman buy herself or her family new clothes or shoes?

3 Do you think all the children receive an education? For how long? How good an education do you think it would be?

4 Do you think that the members of the family are generally in good health? For what sort of illnesses might they require treatment?

5 Describe the house the family lives in. How is it heated? How is it lit? What fuel is used for cooking? If the family cannot afford to buy fuel, what could they use instead? What are the problems getting it? How do you think they obtain water?

6 How much housework do you think the woman has to do?

7 How do you think the woman travels?

8 What sorts of recreation and holidays are available to the family?

9 Could the family meet unexpected expenses, such as house repairs or hospital bills?

10 Overall, what quality of life do you think this woman is able to enjoy?

TOZAMA MAFEKE
HOW SHOULD THE FAMILY'S INCOME OF £40 A MONTH BE SPENT?

Tozama Mafeke. A widow with a baby and two school-age children, who lives with an elderly mother-in-law in one of the 'homelands'. The income of the family is about £40 a month.

DRESS £10-£20

TRANSISTOR £12

CHOCOLATE 43p

BLANKET £5

COKE 52p

SHOES £10-£20

EGGS 80p for 6

RICE 89p for 500g
(will last about
2 days for a family
of 5)

COOKING OIL
£1.79 per 750mls

CANDLES
79p for 6

SOAP 41p

MEAT £3-£5 per
½kg (1 meal)

MILK £1.04 per litre

SAMP (made from
maize, boiled with
beans to make a
favourite main meal
dish) £2.25 per
2½kg (will last
about 5 days for a
family of 5)

TAXES
£1 per month per
adult

MEDICAL FEES
50p (for very basic
medical care)

BUS FARES?

PARAFFIN
(for lighting and
cooking)
£20 per month

A LETTER?

ENTERTAINMENT?

NEWSPAPER?

BICYCLE
£6 per month

JAM £1.45

TEA £1.99

SUGAR £1.15

MARGARINE 99p

PILCHARDS
£1.25 (1 meal)

BABY CEREAL 78p

POWDERED MILK
£3.19 per 500g

TOMATO PUREE 40p

BEANS 99p
for 500g (will last
about 2 days for
family of 5 — good
source of protein)

MAIZE MEAL
£1.88 per 2½kg (will
last about 2 days for
family of 5 — used
for porridge)

FRESH FRUIT AND
VEGETABLES
Best if she can grow
her own — but she
needs seeds,
fertilizer, fencing
and garden
equipment

EDUCATION
£13 school fees per
year per child,
plus books
plus school uniform
plus extra expenses
now and then

N.B. These are 1987 prices, and are approximate, as there is a lot of variation between different regions. Prices in Rands have been translated straight into £s to make it easier for you to deal with them. (The purchasing power of the Rand is, anyway, approximately equal to what £1 will buy in Britain.)

PATTY BROWN

HOW SHOULD THE FAMILY'S INCOME OF £1800 A MONTH BE SPENT?

Patty Brown. Married with two children, she lives in a rich white suburb of Johannesburg. The family's income is about £1800 per month. She is shopping with her domestic worker.

CHOCOLATE 43p

COKE 52p

SOAP 30p

COOKING OIL
£1.79 for 750mls

MEAT £3-£5
per ½kg (1 meal)

MILK £1.04
per litre

CAR £250 per
month H.P.

PETROL £200
per month

MUSSELS 99p
per 250g

DRESS £30-£100

SALARY OF
DOMESTIC WORKER
£80

MEAL IN
RESTAURANT
£20 per person

THEATRE £20
per person

EGGS 80p for 6

RICE 89p for 500g
(will last about
2 days for a family
of 5)

JAM £1.45

TOMATO PUREE 40p

MARGARINE 99p

BABY CEREAL 78p

PILCHARDS £1.20
(1 meal)

BREAD 54p

SUGAR £1.15

TEA £1.99

MACARONI 69p
per 500g

POWDERED MILK
£3.19 per 500g

FRUIT AND
VEGETABLES
£20 per week

CHEESE £3 per kg

WINE £3 per litre

FISH £2.50 per kg

EDUCATION free

SCHOOL UNIFORM
£4 per month if
bought on H.P.

TAXES £258 per
month

NEWSPAPERS £25-£60

STEREO £50
per month if bought
on H.P.

SAVINGS PER MONTH for
one month's holiday at
coast or game reserve or
casino £330

SUBSCRIPTION to sports
club per month £10

MEDICAL FEES
£45 private medical care

TELEPHONE BILL
£100

ELECTRICITY
£200 per month

MORTGAGE
£200-£300

ENTERTAINING FRIENDS
to meals, drinks, evenings
around the pool

N.B. These are 1987 prices, and are approximate, as there is a lot of variation between different regions. Prices in Rands have been translated straight into £s to make it easier for you to deal with them. (The purchasing power of the Rand is, anyway, approximately equal to what £1 will buy in Britain.)

Appendix 3

SACHED (the South African Committee for Higher Education) and Khanya College, both privately funded and oriented to upgrading black students education, have introduced a wide range of exciting new curricula using imaginative teaching resources. They concentrate on small classes and improving study skills. They have produced resource books on the nature of the education system and the exploitation of black women, made imaginative use of a magazine and comic-strip format for getting across a wide range of ideas, run correspondence courses with open access, and entered students for the examinations of the Joint Matriculation Board, a course usually barred to black students. The weekly newspaper **The New Nation** includes an educational supplement, which also introduces a wide range of ideas, not part of the standard syllabi, and special study exercises. Civic associations in many small towns, particularly in the Eastern Cape, have organised self-education projects and established small libraries. Trade unions have included educational work as part of their general organisational efforts.

● **Education.** Action against apartheid education in the form of class boycotts diminished in 1987 as pupils responded to the call by the National Education Crisis Committee to return to class and make the campaign for People's Education a priority. In the Western Cape however there were renewed boycotts in the middle of the year at the closure of schools in protest at teachers being forced to move because they had supported pupil protests. There were also class boycotts when the police shot Ashley Kriel, a former student activist alleged to be an ANC combatant. Throughout the country there were class boycotts in May in protest at the white elections. An Education Laws Amendment Bill published in September was rejected by an NECC conference especially convened to discuss it. It was criticised as an instrument of further government control, and as involving a permanent extension of emergency regulations in law, in particular powers to close down schools and to exclude pupils from educational institutions.

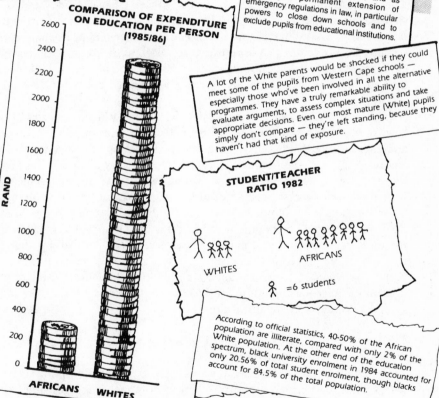

COMPARISON OF EXPENDITURE ON EDUCATION PER PERSON (1985/86)

RAND

AFRICANS   WHITES

A lot of the White parents would be shocked if they could meet some of the pupils from Western Cape schools — especially those who've been involved in all the alternative programmes. They have a truly remarkable ability to evaluate arguments, to assess complex situations and take appropriate decisions. Even our most mature (White) pupils simply don't compare — they're left standing, because they haven't had that kind of exposure.

STUDENT/TEACHER RATIO 1982

WHITES

AFRICANS

♀ =6 students

According to official statistics, 40-50% of the African population are illiterate, compared with only 2% of the White population. At the other end of the education spectrum, black university enrolment in 1984 accounted for only 20.56% of total student enrolment, though blacks account for 84.5% of the total population.

When comparing education we find that blacks are having little education than whites. Even if our education is little this does not mean that we are dull and must be treated like dogs.

Shoitto — 13 years

6 In at the deep end: English and Bengali verse

SIBANI RAYCHAUDHURI

The relationship between European and Asian languages in the UK is strained more than ever after the introduction of the National Curriculum because of its failure to recognize the need for mother-tongue teaching in our schools. In this context, an imaginative approach to the teaching of language awareness of non-European languages in British schools seems both necessary and appropriate, if schools are to pay 'civilized respect' to the other languages of Britain.

In this chapter, I shall try to consider the ways in which the poetry of two languages (English and Bengali) can be used side by side in order to raise the awareness of non-European languages among a group of indigenous pupils and teachers. (By 'indigenous' I mean native speakers of English, although the classes with whom I used these lessons have always included some children for whom English was a second language, because of the multilingual nature of the schools in my area.) Initially, I devised a course for teachers of English in order to point out how difficult it is for a bilingual learner to come to terms with poetry in English unless access is provided by drawing parallels in his or her first language. Later, I used this course as a way of promoting language awareness among middle-school children, using groups of mainly 'indigenous' pupils in the 12–13 year age range.

The following were my broad aims:

1 To reveal to pupils the linguistic diversity represented in the class by speakers of different languages.
2 To reduce pupils' reluctance towards learning a non-European language and to encourage more positive attitudes towards languages other than English.
3 To develop an awareness of pattern, contrast and form, and of various techniques used in the poetry of the two languages as well as to compare and contrast the poetry in the two languages.

4 To promote an appreciation of the difficulties involved in learning through a second language, and to highlight the role of one's first language in learning.

5 To promote an appreciation of different cultures, and to foster better understanding between ethnic groups.

In order to try and achieve these, I attempted the following:

- To bring together the poetry of the two languages. The poem in English I selected was W.H. Auden's 'Night Mail', a poem known to most English teachers and which begins with the following lines:

> This is the Night Mail crossing the Border,
> Bringing the cheque and the postal order.
>
> Letters for the rich, letters for the poor,
> The shop at the corner, the girl next door.
>
> Pulling up Beattock, a steady climb:
> The gradient's against her, but she's on time.
>
> Past cotton-grass and moorland boulder,
> Shovelling white steam over her shoulder.

The Bengali poem was 'Railway Station' ('Istesan') by Rabindranath Tagore (the poem in Bengali script, in the Roman alphabet for enunciation and an English translation can be found in Appendix 1).

- To identify letters, words and sounds.
- To compare the two languages and consider language families, different forms of writing, different scripts/alphabets and the different ways of punctuating scripts.
- To compare the techniques used in the poems in the two languages: the use of rhyme-pattern, onomatopoeia, etc.
- To consider the cultural backgrounds of the poems.
- To consider the use and role of one's first language in learning.

Presentation of the course

Having told the students[1] that they were going to learn another language, the course was presented in three stages.

Stage 1

During this session, only Bengali was spoken. The students were introduced to the Bengali poem 'Istesan' by Rabindranath Tagore in its original Bengali form. Having listened to the sound of the poem and the language as it was read aloud to them, I engaged the students in discussion in Bengali. After about 10 minutes, the students became anxious and restless, and on a couple of occasions a student (in both cases a teacher in fact) left the classroom, finding that he or she was unable to cope with not knowing what was going on. Then I asked them to copy the poem in Bengali script for another 10 minutes. Although the students were initially relieved to find that the task was within their competence, they soon became bored and frustrated because the task was undemanding. Most of the students – both teachers and school-children – copied the poem into Bengali beautifully, but all of them required some kind of help with the directionality of writing and letter formation. These were demonstrated on the blackboard.

Stage 2

The students attended a lesson on Bengali as a second language. Using the *immersion* technique,[2] they were taught some common vocabulary and simple sentences through repetition, aided by pictures and gestures. They were asked to match words and sentences with the appropriate pictures, and they were also asked to draw pictures and label them in Bengali. I rewarded them at every stage if they responded correctly. They seemed to enjoy this session and felt that they had learnt some Bengali, but they soon realized that what they had learnt was quite unrelated to the previous lesson, which had been their mainstream lesson; the content of the language lesson was not appropriate for their age. Once again, the students found the task undemanding. They said that they would become bored if this type of lesson went on for very long. If Bengali had been their second language and they were living in the country where it was the native language and the language of power, they would have been anxious to undertake work appropriate to their age, namely mainstream lessons.

Stage 3

The students were given the following:

- Worksheet I; the poem 'Istesan' in Bengali script, in the Roman alphabet for enunciation and an English translation; an audiotape in Bengali.
- Worksheet II and the English poem 'Night Mail' by W.H. Auden (see Appendix 2 for worksheets).

In a session that lasted about 1 hour, the students were asked to work in groups of four. They found it easier to work on the tasks using their first language, i.e. English. They felt able to cope with the high cognitive demands of the tasks, because they were able to receive instructions in English. They were able to identify rhyming letters and words in Bengali through close observation of the scripts and by carefully listening to the sounds when the poem was read out aloud. They learnt that the rhyme-scheme used in the Bengali poem was the same as in the English poem. They also identified the use of onomatopoeia in the Bengali poem, where it is used to give the sound of a train: they found the equivalent English onomatopoeia in 'Railway Station' (English translation). The word 'Istesan', a loan word in Bengali (from 'station' in English), led to a discussion of word-borrowing between the two languages, as a result of language-contact during British rule in the Indian subcontinent. This is an important way language changes, by absorbing words from other languages and cultures. Then the students made a list of loan words in English borrowed from the languages of the Indian subcontinent. I also presented a list of loan words in Bengali that came from English:

Loan words in Bengali from English		Loan words in English from Indian languages
English	Bengali	
out	aut	loot
apple	apel	thug
box	bakso	yoga
office	ap(h)is	dekko
inch	inchi	pukka(h)
station	istesan	veranda
school	iskul	dinghy
cornice	karnis	cheetah
guardian	garzen	chapati
tile	tali	pundit
ticket	tikit	pyjamas
double	dobol	curry
police	pulis	
bench	benchi	

At a higher level, the students (mainly teachers) were able to engage in an interpretation of the poem. By and large, their interpretations corresponded to William Radice's (1985): 'The core of the poem lies in the vision of the coming and going of the station as nothing more than *calacchabi* or *calti cchabi*, "moving pictures", i.e. an insubstantial, unreal, arbitrary sequence of painted images.' At this point, the students began to search for background information to Tagore's poetry, which led them to consider the influence of the Upanishadic philosophy: for Tagore, painting is often associated with the unreal, a state of alienation caused by separation from the reality of God or Brahman. 'Istesan' or 'Railway Station' is a vision of life with its essential reality left out; it presents a sense of alienation, a sense of boredom on the part of the speaker in the poem. I should mention here that there were a few Bengali students in the groups, who drew upon their knowledge of language, culture and philosophy wherever possible. Non-Bengali students from the subcontinent also found themselves in the position of comparative experts as far as the cultural connotations of the poem were concerned.

With Auden's poem 'Night Mail', all the indigenous students felt secure and confident simply because the poem was in English and because of their familiarity with its cultural assumptions, although some needed help in understanding the meaning of words like 'Beattock', 'cotton-grass', etc. This led to a sense of how language changes over a period of time and how language varies from one region to another – and from one class to another.

The students found certain features common to both poems:

- Both poems imitate the sound of a moving train.
- Both poems have the same rhyme-scheme, i.e. they are both written in rhyming couplets.
- Both poems present pictures of life and the surrounding world, but Tagore's poem is more philosophical in nature.

This language awareness course was a deliberate attempt to eliminate linguistic racism and break down the cultural intolerance which prevails because of lack of knowledge combined with a sense of insecurity. Through this course, I tried to open the students' minds and to encourage them to be inquisitive and receptive to new sounds, speech patterns, alphabets, writing systems and to the culture a particular language reflects. My aim was to build up the students' confidence in making comparisons across two languages, and in accepting the universals of human language.

This course could also be used to prepare and motivate students to learn a second language and also to see an unfamiliar language in the light of their own. There is a particular implication for teachers of bilingual learners: the crucial role that the students' first language plays in learning a second language. Also, in the early stages of learning a new language, both adults and adolescents lean heavily on written materials in their first language. This supports Vygotsky's analysis of the central role literacy plays in the interaction of first- and second-language development. This dependency on the first language and its semantic system in the learning of a second language is supposed to deepen the learner's knowledge of the first language. The deepened knowledge of the first language helps learners to develop their metalinguistic awareness, and enables them to compare and contrast their first language with the second language. By this means effective second-language learning takes place. This also points to the effectiveness of mother-tongue teaching for bilingual learners if it takes place along the same lines as mainstream English teaching. In this way, English and the mother-tongue interact with each other and sustain each other.

> If pupils come to school with a skill in a language other than English (here it is Bengali), then that skill needs to be used for that child's intellectual and educational development. If English and Bengali are brought into an interactive relationship so that the pupil can use both languages to learn, we are some way towards encouraging bilingual development and skills of bilingualism.

Being able to relate one language to another and interpret one culture to someone from another culture are also skills of bilingualism.

(Raychaudhuri and Read, 1990: 4)

Notes

1 So as to avoid confusion, I use the term 'students', although I used this course with both teachers and schoolchildren.
2 'Immersion' refers to a situation in which students from the same linguistic and cultural background are taught together in a class where a second language other than their mother-tongue is used as the medium of instruction.

References

Auden, W.H. (1966). Night Mail. In Auden, W.H., *Collected Shorter Poems*. London: Faber.
Cummins, J. and Swain, M. (1984). *Bilingualism in Education*. London: Longman.
Department of Education and Science (1988). *Report of the Committee of Inquiry into the Teaching of English Language* (The Kingman Report). London: HMSO.
Department of Education and Science (1989). *English for Ages 5 to 16* (The Cox Report). London: DES and the Welsh Office.
Donmall, G. (ed.) (1985). *Language Awareness*, NCLE Papers and Reports 6. London: CILT.
Hawkins, E. (1984). *Awareness of Language: An Introduction*. Cambridge: Cambridge University Press.
Radice, W. (1985). *Rabindranath Tagore: Selected Poems*. Harmondsworth: Penguin.
Raychaudhuri, S. and Read, R. (1990). *Bengali Poetry, English Poetry*. London: Kavita Publications.
Reid, E. (ed.) (1984). *Minority Community Languages in School*, NCLE Papers and Reports 4. London: CILT.
Tagore, R. (1940). istésan. In *Naba-jātak*. Calcutta, India: Visva Bharati.
Wertsch, J.V. (ed.) (1985). *Culture, Communication and Cognition: Vygotskyan Perspectives*. Cambridge: Cambridge University Press.

Appendix 1

Roman alphabet version of 'Istesan'

This is not phonetically transcribed.

Istesan

Sokal bikal istatione asi,
chae chae dekte bhalobasi,
basto hoee ora ticket kene;
bhnatir traine keou ba chare, keou ba ujan traine.
sokal theke keou ba thake bose,
keou ba garhi fel kare tar shes minuter doshe

dinrat garh – garh – gharh – gharh
garhi – bhora manuser chhote jhar.
ghana ghana gati tar ghurbe
Kabhu paschime kabhu purbe.

chalachhabir ei-je murtikhani
monete dei ani
nitya-melar nitya-bholar bhasa –
kebal jaoa-asa.
manchatale dande pale bhirh jama hai kato –
patakata dei dulie, ke kotha hoi gata!
er pichhane sukh dukha khati labher tarha
dei sabole narha
samayer gharhi-dhara ankate
bhno bhno kare bansi baje sankete
deri nahi sai karo kichhutei -
keha jai, keha thake pichhutei.

Oder chaler oder parhe thakai
aar kichhu nei, chhabir pare kebal chhabi ankai.
khanikkhan ja chokhe parhe tar pare jai muchhe,
atma-obohelar khela nityai jai ghuchhe.
chhera poter tukro jame pather pranto jure,
tapto diner klanto haoay konkhane jai ure.
'galo galo' bole jara fukre knede othe
khanek-pare kanna-samet tarai pichhe chhote. –
dhong dhong baje uthe ghanta,
ese pare bidayer khanta.
mukh rakhe janlai barie,
nimisei nie jai chharie.
by Rabindranath Tagore

'Istesan' in English

Railway Station

I come to the station morning and evening,
I love to watch the coming and going –
Hubbub of passengers pressing for tickets,
Down-trains boarded, up-trains boarded,
Ebb and flow like an estuarine river.
Some people sitting there ever since morning,
Other people missing their train by a minute.

Day – Night – clanking and rumbling,
Trainloads of people thundering forth.
On and on with repetitive movement,
Eastwards, westwards, rapid as storms.

The essence of all these moving pictures
Brings to my mind the image of language,
Forever forming, forever unforming,
Continuous coming, continuous going.
Crowds can fill the stage in an instant –
The guard's flag waves the train's departure
And suddenly everyone disappears somewhere.
The hurry disguises their joys and sorrows,
Masks the pressure of gains and losses.

> Bho – Bho – blows the whistle,
> Sounding the clock's division of time.
> The train is indifferent to anyone's lateness,
> Some will go, some stay behind.

Coming and going, leaving and remaining,
   Nothing but picture after picture.
Whatever catches the eye for a moment
   Is erased the next moment after.
A whimsical game, a self-forgetting
   Ever-dissolving sequence –
Each canvas ripped, its shreds discarded
   To pile up along the roadside,
Detritus lifted hither and thither
   By tired hot summer breezes.
'It's gone, it's gone,' rings out the clamour
   Of passengers left stranded –
Next thing they have also vanished,
   Chasing, running, wailing.

> Clang – Clang – sounds the tocsin,
> Time for good-bye, off goes the train.
> Passengers leaning out of the windows,
> Waving until they are whisked away.
>   Rabindranath Tagore

Bengali script of istésan

ইস্টেশন

–রবীন্দ্রনাথ ঠাকুর

সকাল বিকাল ইস্টেশনে আসি,
চেয়ে চেয়ে দেখতে ভালোবাসি,
ব্যস্ত হয়ে ওরা টিকিট কেনে;
ভাঁটির ট্রেনে কেউ বা চড়ে, কেউ বা উজান ট্রেনে।
সকাল থেকে কেউ বা থাকে বসে,
কেউ বা গাড়ি ফেল করে তার শেষ মিনিটের দোষে।–
দিনরাত গড়ু গড়ু ঘড়ু ঘড়ু
গাড়ি-ভরা মানুষের ছোটে ঝড়।
ঘন ঘন গতি তার ঘুরবে
কভু পশ্চিমে কভু পূর্বে।
চলচ্ছবির এই-যে মূর্তিখানি
মনেতে দেয় আনি
নিত্য-মেলার নিত্য-ভোলার ভাষা–
কেবল যাওয়া আসা।
মঞ্চতলে দণ্ডে পলে ভিড় জমা হয় কত–
পতাকাটা দেয় দুলিয়ে, কে কোথা হয় গত।
এর পিছনে সুখ দুঃখ ক্ষতি লাভের তাড়া
দেয় সবলে নাড়া।–
সময়ের ঘড়ি-ধরা অঙ্কেতে
ভোঁ ভোঁ ক'রে বাঁশি বাজে সংকেতে।
দেরি নাহি সয় কারো কিছুতেই–
কেহ যায়, কেহ থাকে পিছুতেই।
ওদের চলা ওদের প'ড়ে থাকায়
আর কিছু নেই, ছবির পরে কেবল ছবি আঁকায়।
খানিক্ষণ যা চোখে পড়ে তার পরে যায় মুছে,
আত্ম –অবহেলার খেলা নিত্যই যায় ঘুচে।
ছেঁড়া পটের টুকরো জমে পথের প্রান্ত জুড়ে,
তপ্ত দিনের ক্লান্ত হাওয়ায় কোনখানে যায় উড়ে।
'গেল গেল' ব'লে যারা ফুক্‌রে কেঁদে ওঠে
ক্ষণেক-পরে কান্না-সমেত তারাই পিছে ছোটে।–
ঢং ঢং বেজে ওঠে ঘন্টা,
এসে পড়ে বিদায়ের ক্ষণটা।
মুখ রাখে জানালায় বাড়িয়ে,
নিমিষেই নিয়ে যায় ছাড়িয়ে।

Appendix 2

Worksheet I

Answer in Bengali or in your own language:

1 Read the English translation twice.
2 Listen to the poem in Bengali on the tape.
3 Listen to the tape again. This time, try to follow the words on the page.
4 Now, from the Bengali version find the words that rhyme. Underline the words that rhyme.
  Suggest the rhyme scheme.
  Work out the punctuation in the text.
  Work out the directionality of the script.
5 Underline the sound words (onomatopoeia) in the Bengali version.
6 Suggest a title for the poem.
7 What is the poem about? Write a paragraph about the poem.
8 Identify the following words in Bengali and write them down
  morning   day   down-train
  evening   night   up-trains

Worksheet II

1 Now, read the poem 'Night Mail'.
  What is the poem about?
  Write a paragraph about the poem.
2 Do these two poems have anything in common?
3 What do you *understand* by the following words?
  Night Mail
  Border
  Beattock
  Cotton-grass
  moorland
  Sheep dog
  a glade of cranes
  glens/lochs

7 'Can you fully understand it?': Approaching issues of racism with white students in the English classroom[1]

BEVERLEY NAIDOO

You sort of get right down deep in yourself and pull out all the answers.

It makes you ask things that you don't really understand.

When people who are hot-seated are asked questions they seem to have answers that you never thought of.

These comments by three 14-year-old students suggest a learning experience which has been personal, active and exploratory. Their discussion, which focused on the technique of 'hot-seating' characters from the novel they were reading, followed directly on from an English session with writer Millie Murray. With considerable versatility, Millie had been answering questions in the role of three central female characters from Mildred Taylor's *Roll of Thunder, Hear My Cry*. Seen through the eyes of young Cassie Logan, the events in this novel are a powerful portrayal of black experience in the American south of the 1930s. First as Cassie, then with her hair up as her mother, and finally wearing a head-scarf as her grandmother, Millie had engaged the class of thirty 13- and 14-year-olds for over an hour with her rendering of the three generations.

A distinctive feature of the occasion was that apart from Millie Murray, the participants were all white. These students attended a Church comprehensive in a relatively prosperous urban area of Britain with a largely white population. They were part of the 'middle band' of a school where, despite European diversity, all but half a dozen of the 1200 pupils were white. For these students, it was the first time they had been offered in class a novel written by a black author – and the first time they had been challenged in any sustained way to consider experience from a black perspective. Given the limits of their own environment and culture, how would they understand the text? It was not simply that the novel demanded a leap back in time and across the Atlantic. Their experience of American films and access to white American culture would probably enable such leaps to be made with ease where protagonists and perspectives remained largely white. But what knowledge did they have of black history and experience – and how would this affect their responses to the novel? In this context, Millie's particular brief was not only to elicit questions from the class about 'things that you don't really understand', but through her responses to challenge misconceptions, i.e. to suggest those 'answers that you never thought of'. Could she, by what she said and portrayed, begin to disturb some of the mental underpinning for complacency about racism? A tall order for a single session.

However, this was part of a year-long project (commencing September 1988) on exploring issues of racism with white students through fiction and drama. Quantitative data on racist/non-racist perceptions, assumptions, values and beliefs were collected through a survey before and after the project, but the study was largely ethnographic and qualitative. Apart from a few occasions when the teacher was absent, I maintained a non-teaching role as a participant observer. On average, two out of the week's four 50-minute English lessons were devoted to the selected literature and related activities. A weekly drama lesson linked to the project was attended by alternating halves of the class.

Data on the students' responses were collected in diverse forms. All of the lessons and small group discussions were tape-recorded. The students kept reading journals in which they were encouraged to jot down initial impressions, thoughts and feelings as well as later reflections. Sometimes they were asked to make immediate jottings around a particular passage or poem on a printed sheet. Further data were gathered through interviews with the students and the teacher. An important area for enquiry was the context in which the texts were being experienced – beginning with that of the classroom and the learning environment created by the teacher.

The literature course itself was carefully designed to explore the students' understandings of, and responses to, racism in a variety of contexts, progressively homing in to Britain. The works chosen not only had to meet the school's traditional literary criteria for what would be regarded as suitable year 9 texts, but needed to reflect perspectives which strongly indicated racism. Although the first novel, Nigel Hinton's Buddy, is set in Britain, questions of racism within it are only a side issue. Nevertheless, it was a book to which the students could easily relate, allowing me general observation as well as an opportunity for mapping initial levels of awareness to the dimension of racism within the text. Next came Hans Peter Richter's *Friedrich*, set in Germany in the 1930s, intended to encourage exploration of racism in a European context. It was only in the second term, however, that issues of domination and resistance in relation to colour developed a major focus through Mildred Taylor's *Roll of Thunder, Hear My Cry*, followed by Sheila Gordon's South African novel *Waiting for the Rain*. Reading these novels took longer than predicted, resulting in much reduced time for British literature. Some poetry was read, as well as Farrukh Dhondy's story *K.B.W.* (short for 'Keep Britain White'). However, at this stage the issues began to be overtly addressed in a series of religious education lessons where the students watched and discussed the BBC education series *Getting to Grips with Racism*. Throughout the course, an attempt was made to relate the literature to the social context out of which it had arisen, particularly through the use of video material and recorded author-interviews.

A further significant feature of the project was the opportunity of direct contact with black artists. These sessions took different forms, from drama workshops with Richard Finch on themes related to *Friedrich* and Nazi Germany, hot-seating sessions alongside drama and writing workshops with Millie Murray, a poetry reading by James Berry, and finally a week of daily workshops with dramatist/director Olusola Oyeleye.

Throughout the year, my concern was to map out the students' 'frames of reference' (Figueroa, 1984), so as to ascertain the 'largely taken for granted understandings, which . . . provide as it were a basic "backdrop" to perception, knowledge, judgement and action'. I wanted to gain some idea of the lenses through which the students were perceiving and filtering the various texts and related experiences. I hoped also to be able to observe any signs of possible reframing of these lenses. As a writer, Mildred Taylor herself has acknowledged concern with reframing perceptions:

> I wanted to show a different kind of black world from the one so often seen. I wanted to show a family united in love and self-respect, and parents strong and sensitive, attempting to guide their children successfully without harming their spirits, through the hazardous maze of living in a discriminatory society.
>
> I also wanted to show the black person as heroic. In my own school days, a class devoted to the history of black people in the United States always caused me painful embarrassment . . . the indictment of slavery was also an indictment of the people who were enslaved – a people who, according to the texts, were docile and childlike, accepting their fate without once attempting to free themselves . . . I used to sit tensely waiting out those class hours trying to think of ways to repudiate what the textbooks said, for I recognized that there was a terrible contradiction between what was in them and what I had learned at home.
>
> It is my hope that to the children who read my books, the Logans will provide the heroes missing from the schoolbooks of my childhood, black men, women and children of whom they can be proud.
>
> (Taylor, 1977: 15)

Aspirations such as these were central to the idea of inviting Millie Murray to take on the roles of various black characters from the texts. We began with Charmian from *Buddy*, the idea germinating after I had observed a hot-seating session among the students themselves. Buddy, a white working-class boy whose mother has walked out, is trapped between the expectations of a wayward Teddy Boy father and those of the 'Express' stream at school. His only friends are the twins Charmian and Julius, likewise outsiders, but they are black. Hot-seating as Buddy, Ian[2] – a student holding a wide range of racist views and one of the highest scorers on the survey of racist perceptions – felt it necessary to justify the friendship: 'Because they sort of show me that they're not really black. They're sort of the same as me.'

Did any of the other students also perhaps hold 'whitened' images of the twins? Further evidence of an essentially negative perception relating to black people came from a girl who was one of the lowest scorers on the survey. Angela was the most outspoken, self-confident girl in the class, articulating strong views on equality. Irish born, she spoke Southern British Standard English, declaring boldly in the survey: 'I think about how lucky I am to be Irish and I am never ashamed.' Nevertheless, Angela role-played Charmian as passively putting up with racism, rather than reacting with any anger:

> *Donald*: What do you think about all the other kids in your class, how they treat you?
> *Angela*: Oh I just shrug it off. You get used to it after a while. I mean quite a lot of kids are racist I suppose. I mean I've got my brother . . my twin to stick with so I don't really mind . . .[3]
> *Terry*: If Buddy asked you out what would you say?
> *Angela*: I'd probably say yes, but he'd probably get a lot of stick from all the other white kids, so if it was for his sake I'd say no.

Asked about her parents, she spoke of them being supportive and 'jolly', cheering her up when necessary, but admitted to feeling shame at times:

> *Teacher*: Are you sometimes embarrassed by them (your parents) in the way Buddy is sometimes embarrassed by his father?
> *Angela*: I don't think in the same way. I mean I don't mind their taste in things. Sometimes I get ashamed of my colour and their colour.
> *Teacher*: Why?
> *Angela*: Because although people say that my mother is really jolly and she reflects on people and makes them happy and things, sometimes when we are walking together people give her funny looks and things.

This interpretation of Charmian seemed in marked contrast to Angela's stated pride in her own origins and was not grounded in the text. Charmian is not present when the racist joking takes place, nor do we hear any commentary from her on it. Whenever we see her, she is confident, caring and perceptive. The ways that Angela filled the gaps in the text (Iser, 1978) and the sort of predictions she made suggested significant cultural stereotyping which needed to be challenged.

Once Millie Murray had agreed to be hot-seated – as Charmian, speaking Standard English, and as her mother, Mrs Rybeero, speaking Creole – the students were asked if they would like to meet the two of them 10 years on from the book. Initial scepticism about a 'real' Charmian soon turned to enthusiasm. The class wrote down their expectations of what Charmian might now be like and potential questions for the visitors. Millie was sent these, with a copy of the students' own hot-seating session, giving her an idea of the implicit stereotypes she would attempt to counter.

Further drama work focused on status and power, the students again being asked to fill a gap in the text by improvising the scene on Parents' Evening between the racist teacher Mr Normington and the Rybeeros. Angela, playing Mrs Rybeero, hotly defended her son but didn't raise the issue of racism. However, in the following week's improvisation, an astute boy called Philip, playing Mr Rybeero, openly confronted Mr Normington (played by the teacher):

> *Philip*:   Can you explain why you complain when Charmian is being quiet and you complain when her brother is the opposite? Would you prefer them both to be dumb?
>
> *Teacher*:   No Mr Rybeero. What I am asking is for Julian to think before he speaks and Carmian [*sic*] to speak at all. I would appreciate it if you would say something to them about this. (The teacher deliberately mispronouncing the twins' names)
>
> *Philip*:   I just think Charmian is intimidated by whites. If you go into any High Street white people will take the micky out of her.

The meeting ended, however, with Mr Normington slickly defusing the conflict, with general agreement from the students that this role-play seemed realistic. Sympathy clearly rested with the Rybeeros who had been out-manipulated, but they nevertheless remained framed in terms of 'intimidated victims'.

There were also signs that common stereotypes and fears could be tapped without much difficulty. This emerged in a discussion about Buddy's sense of awkwardness at the Satellite Youth Club, most of whose members were black. The teacher queried whether it was simply shyness about entering a crowd:

> *Simon*:   I think it's because he . . he doesn't know anybody else there . . if you know he's in a sort of very, *very* strange environment . . like and they're all coloured people in there. If it was a white Youth Club then I think he would find it a bit easier to go into.
>   . . .
> *John*:   If it was me I don't think I would have . . I would have even tried to go in there.
> *Teacher*:   Why not?
> *John*:   I'd feel too out of place and all these black people looking at you and people staring . . . I'd be frightened what to say.

When the teacher turned the discussion to Dennis, a black friend of Julius who is hostile to Buddy – having had 'a bit of bother from some white kids at his school' (p. 21) – I felt some students begin to voice disquiet at a potential focus on themselves alongside Buddy:

Jacky: He kind of thinks that all white kids will be against him as well.

Ian (who in role as Buddy had said the twins were 'not really black') certainly felt the rub. His statement provides a clear example of projection, one of the prime 'devices for guilt-evasion' (Allport, 1979):

Ian: Well he's sort of a typical black because they sort of judge you as how they judge their friends and you're a different colour and they think that you make racialist remarks about them whatever. They think you're in a sort of gang, who sort of make remarks about them.

Initially, almost all of the students were taken in by Millie's Charmian, presented as a resourceful, articulate writer who – reflecting Millie's own career – had been a psychiatric nurse and a secretary. Suspicions were only aroused when she re-appeared as a motherly, outspoken Mrs Rybeero, whose sharp tongue reduced Mr Normington to 'that wicked, evil man!' This part of the session was peppered with laughter, largely at Millie's versatile parrying of questions aimed at detecting her true identity. Through both characters, however, Millie introduced a range of challenging attitudes.

Asked about the racist jokes in the 'Express' class, Millie's Charmian combined perceptive sympathy for Buddy's desire not to be an outcast with contempt for the initiators of the racism who:

... didn't openly come out .. and that gave me strength. I felt good about that .. because that's what bullies are like you know people who are racist who have these racist attitudes .. making snide remarks .. they could never come up and say 'you jungle-bunny' .. as you walk by you catch it but you're walking by . . .

Reflecting on Mr Normington's 'man-made air of self-importance', she made it clear that although Charmian had not been able to confront him as a child, this did not imply getting 'used to' the abuse:

... the snide remarks he used to make about my colour I um found very offensive .. but you know .. it's not something .. really that .. you can um dwell on too much .. because I think it could make you quite violent actually .. you know if somebody never liked you because of your colour or . . . you spoke differently or . . . you come from a place that's different from them or your eyes are blue or your religion is different .. you know I find that incredible .. that people can dislike you because of that .. you know it's very very sad .. so .. now on reflection when I think of Mr Normington .. I do feel angry at times when I think of all the times when I really could have stood up to him but .. I pity him .. because he obviously has a problem .. to be that way to young people. I wonder if he would be that way perhaps .. to a black man .. you know on an equal level to him .. perhaps not.

Mr Normington's abuse of power had not ultimately won the day – either by provoking Charmian to 'dwell on' it too much in sheer anger, or by accepting the demeaning message. Indeed the provocation seemed to have encouraged Millie's Charmian to become more resilient. She was able to see Mr Normington in terms of a wider human canvas. By relating his racism to other kinds of discrimination and particularly to his domination of young people, Millie opened out a number of links for her audience to consider.

Responding to questions on a range of issues (including what it's like to be featured in a book!), Millie's Charmian and Mrs Rybeero were not one-dimensional 'victims', but individuals contending with – and resisting – racism as part of full, active lives.

Coming out of role, Millie initiated small group drama work. Given a fictional entry in Charmian's diary about Mr Normington endorsing yet more racist baiting, the students were asked to improvise a subsequent scene with Charmian and friends. It was a task they found difficult, Millie intervening at one point to ask them how they would feel if the discrimination was against their religion. In a short debriefing, the teacher commented that they conveyed a sense of powerlessness in dealing with the harassment.

The session concluded with a version of Forum Theatre with Millie as Charmian, aged 24, unexpectedly meeting Mr Normington, played by Philip. Other students, sitting in a circle around the two main protagonists, volunteered to be various characters from the book. As the confrontation developed, Charmian and Mr Normington each called on people to speak in their defence. Philip (who as Mr Rybeero had made an able attempt to stand up to the teacher's Mr Normington) quickly found himself overpowered by Charmian's direct accusations with her open, dogged insistence that he had allowed racism to go unchallenged in his classroom. The discussion became increasingly heated, with Donald suddenly accusing Charmian of fabricating evidence because she had a 'chip on her shoulder'. Her reply was straightforward: 'My memory is very good and I haven't got a problem. You see the reason you told me I've got a problem you see is because you're not black.' Unfortunately, further developments were cut short by the bell.

Discussions the following day both in groups and as the whole class were revealing. The assumptions about black women held by Ian and John (the two highest scorers on the survey of racist perceptions) – concerning fertility and achievement – had certainly been challenged, although there was no indication they would be altered. Indeed, two-thirds of the class had predicted Charmian would be married and almost half that she would have children:

> *Tania:* I thought Charmian would be . . would have a family by now.
> *Ian:*   I think it's really um . . that you think of her from a Jamaican I
>   think . . you see um . . quite a lot of black children around so I thought
>   she would have started a family up already.

Tania's response can probably be interpreted in the light of a Christian focus on women as mothers, or her own love of children (wanting to work with them), although in an interview she didn't see herself starting a family: 'It's too much responsibility.' Ian, however, openly admitted to having thought of Charmian 'from a Jamaican'. Later, apparently egged on by Ian, John acknowledged his surprise at Millie being a writer. The giggles and intonation of the exchange suggest an awareness among the group of the racist connotations:

Ian:	I think John wants to say something now!
John:	(brief giggle) I was surprised when um the school got an author . . I thought they would have just got a black woman off the streets . . you know someone they knew or something. (controlling giggle)
Angela:	Oh no! (laughter)
Ian:	That's not very nice! (loud, possibly to convey affected shock)
John:	No! Not off the streets! But someone the school knew (giggle) or somebody like that! (controls laugh)
Neil:	No I don't think so John . . I mean –
John:	I was surprised when they got an author though.
Neil:	It's supposed to be pretty organized! They wouldn't just sort of go out and say 'Would you like to come and do that?'

In contrast, a student scoring at the lowest end of the survey affirmed in another group how much he had enjoyed supporting Charmian in her exchange with Mr Normington. Marco, with an Italian father and English mother – having come from Italy three years previously – refrained from speaking of his own experiences, but commented: 'I suppose you get the same kind of situation if somebody was Irish.' Some months later, in private, he spoke of his personal shock at having been 'put down' as an Italian by a particular teacher.

A number of students acknowledged that the experience had brought new realizations to them about the hurt caused by racist name-calling:

Philip:	I thought it was good 'cause um . . we didn't really understand how blacks feel when they are called racist things . . and we had to try and understand . . (slowing down speech for last phrase – affected?)
Dan:	I think we understood how black people cope . . when they . . when um people make racist remarks at them . . and I think we just . . we just *think* we know what they do . . when they get back . . but . . they really feel . . hurt.
Marian:	But we will never know how they really feel because we are not black ourselves so we will never get the racist remarks that they get . . so . . we won't know exactly.
Caroline:	Yeah but we had a good practice when we were doing the um . . the acting out . . it was pretty good . . we learnt a lot.

Similar sentiments were expressed by others, for example Simon: 'I still think that er . . I didn't realise how much the um black people felt offended by it.' However, Simon was unable to share Michelle's acknowledgement that she now had a better understanding of Dennis' hostile response to Buddy:

> *Michelle*: . . . now I realize that he'd been having . . you know he's been having all this trouble from you know the white kids at school . . . and so now I realize . . . why he was so off to um Buddy.
>
> *Simon*: I understand how Dennis feels but I don't know why he took it out on Buddy . . .
>
> *Andrew*: But at least there's not . . not very much racialism in this school. ('I'm saying the right thing' tone?)

It is difficult to pinpoint undercurrents of tone, but none the less I thought it worth recording where the way in which a statement was said suggested it might have been made simply for public consumption. Andrew had lived in South Africa for a number of years and was therefore likely to be more aware than most of the challenge Millie presented to racist ideas. Certainly there was the potential for him to feel more uncomfortable than most. Apart from a couple of occasions in small group discussion where he ended up more or less defending apartheid and his family's right to have a black servant at the bottom of their garden, I had the feeling he generally kept such challenges at bay by consciously saying the 'right' thing. In the class discussion that followed group talk on Millie's session, the teacher homed in on Andrew:

> *Teacher*: Did it do anything to your um attitudes?
>
> *Andrew*: Yes.
>
> *Teacher*: What?
>
> *Andrew*: Um . . what do you mean by um you know . . .
>
> *Teacher*: Have you ever been in a position where you've had um a black person speaking to you in that way before?
>
> *Andrew*: N-n-
>
> *Teacher*: . . . addressing you in that way before?
>
> *Andrew*: N-no. Not as I can recall . . no.
>
> *Teacher*: Did it surprise you? (Andrew nods) What?
>
> *Andrew*: Um how straightforward she was and you know started to talk just talked about it like um normally like a normal person.

Here Andrew unwittingly revealed that black people for him usually came into a category other than normal. It is impossible to know what lasting effect Millie's visit might have on his frames of reference. He may possibly now concede some black people to be 'normal', while still maintaining that the 'garden-boy' in South Africa was happy working for his family and living at the bottom of their garden.

A number of students made the point that Millie had expected a lot of them. While there is no evidence that they would have commented differently had Millie been white, I hoped this had challenged black 'deficit' imagery. Generally, there was considerable appreciation of the experience Millie had created, as expressed here by Gaby and Julia:

> Gaby: I thought it was good of her to talk about her race and everything 'cause it sort of broke the barrier down.

> [Journal entry by Julia] The work we had to do was good fun and it realized to me how much whites are racist before then I never bothered. Charmian answered all questions well and I thought she had a good ambition.

The opportunity for Millie to return arose a few months later, with *Roll of Thunder, Hear My Cry*. Once again discussion and hot-seating among the students themselves revealed some significant misperceptions. In particular, I was concerned that the Logan children were being regarded as harsh for not accepting the white boy Jeremy's offers of friendship. A common view seemed to be: 'If he is loyal to them, why aren't they loyal to him?' Making judgements from within the confines of their own experience, they seemed to have little idea of the enormous power divide between white and black in America of the 1930s.

In preparation for Millie's session – and to give her an idea of their perceptions – the students were asked to draft film-scripts entitled 'The Burning'. Their brief was to develop a dialogue between Cassie and Jeremy after Cassie suspects his family of involvement in burning a neighbour's house. Only a few of these scripts depicted the confrontation with real tension.

As described earlier, Millie took the students through the three generations of women, changing hairstyle and intonation for each. She then created a short improvisation with a student in the role of Jeremy, using the same starting point as the film-script. As in many of the scripts, Jeremy (played by Peter) sought to gain Cassie's sympathy and 'just be friends' – at first defending his racist father, before saying that he couldn't do anything to change him. Millie, in the role of Cassie, however, refused to let Peter off the hook, forcing him to admit that if his father insisted, he would accompany him on a burning expedition. The scene ended with Cassie expressing disgust. How could they be friends on that basis? In the writing workshop that followed, Peter diverged from the task set by Millie, to produce a piece in role as Jeremy which was impressive not only for its authentic tone of voice ('My Papa sure scares me 'bout the other night'), but as a statement about how he *would* make a stand against his father. Usually fairly reticent, Peter volunteered to read this to the class. It seemed he had become involved in more than an exercise.

Although their journal entries revealed that the students had enjoyed this session, there was a feeling the *Buddy* event had been more fun. Certainly, the majority of questions to Millie on *Roll of Thunder* concerned serious issues, in which racism had shifted centre-stage. However, it was also felt that it would have been good to have been involved in more drama themselves,

Simon commenting that 'I find that when drama is being carried out. I usually understand what is happening better.'

Hot-seating was just one of the drama methods employed during the year's course. The earlier quotations from students point to some of its strengths in encouraging an active response to exploring texts. A further asset is that it can be used as easily in a classroom as in a drama studio. However, it is necessary for participants to recognize its limitations and sensitive debriefing is essential. First, when students are being hot-seated, basic misunderstandings or misreadings of the text may be revealed! Secondly, the tension of being hot-seated may provoke too simplistic, ready-made answers and these need to be questioned. Thirdly, discussion can reveal how a character portrayed through hot-seating is itself a construction, derived not only from the text but from the life experiences of the person in the chair. There would have been great value in more time spent after Millie's sessions contrasting her responses with those given previously by students. How was it that her portrayals were so much fuller? Some would have said she was an adult and an excellent actress. But I would say the chief connection to be made was with her own life experience as a black person in a society where racism remains endemic.

At its best, hot-seating can provide close insight into the 'transaction' between reader and text, in the sense used by Louise Rosenblatt (1985), that 'the reader brings to the text a network of past experiences in literature and in life'. The author, too, brings his or her own such networks to the text, to be distinguished from the 'poem' or 'event' evoked by the reader – 'a lived-through process or experience' (Rosenblatt, 1985).

Hot-seating can provide a dramatic window onto that process of evocation. Hopefully, Millie's strong evocation of various black characters will have facilitated shifts in some of the students' 'frames of reference' – away from stereotype to a fuller reality. But how, when most of us most of the time do not have access to someone like Millie, can we provide a creative challenge to those readers whose realization of characters and situations may be limited by their own narrow set of lenses? Constructive discussion arising out of hot-seating may well lead the students themselves to want to widen their interpretation of a character, and for someone else to volunteer another rendering through further hot-seating. It may be that they need to explore possibilities of response through a different character in a situation to which they feel closer, perhaps from another book, short story or television drama. It may be appropriate to introduce poetry which conveys something of the 'voice' the students may have been missing. The students could be encouraged to explore the poetry and their responses to it through making their own dramatic renderings. There are many poems – including Maya Angelou's wonderful 'And Still I Rise' – which might open the door for students to experience the celebratory sense of resistance of people who have not allowed themselves to become dehumanized by racism.

Whatever the ways in which we attempt to open up such doors, perhaps for ourselves as well as for our students, Millie posed a final question during her second workshop which suggests to me not only the human condition, but the continuing challenge: 'You know unless you are sort of living under oppression of any kind, can you fully understand it?'

Notes

1 I use the terms 'black' and 'white' in the sociopolitical sense where 'black' refers broadly to those people sharing the common experience of racism related to colour.
2 All names of students have been changed.
3 Transcription note:
   .. indicates a pause in speech;
   ... indicates a speech omitted.

References

Allport, G.W. (1979). *The Nature of Prejudice*. Reading, Mass.: Addison-Wesley.
Figueroa, P. (1984). Race relations and cultural differences: Some ideas on racist frames of reference. In Verma, G.K. and Bagley, C. (eds), *Race Relations and Cultural Differences*. London: Croom Helm.
Iser, W. (1978). *The Act of Reading*. London: Routledge and Kegan Paul.
Rosenblatt, L. (1985). The transactional theory of the literary work: Implications for research. In Cooper, C.R. (ed.), *Researching Response to Literature and the Teaching of Literature*. Norwood, N.J.: Ablex.
Taylor, M.D. (1977). Acceptance Speech for the Newbery Award – quoted in an English Centre-booklet on *Roll of Thunder, Hear My Cry*. London: English Centre (1984: available through NATE, Birley School Annexe, Fox Lane, Frechville, Sheffield S12 4WY, UK).

Novels used on the course
Gordon, S. (1987). *Waiting for the Rain*. London: Orchard Books.
Hinton, N. (1983). *Buddy*. London: Heinemann New Windmill.
Richter, H.P. (1978). *Friedrich*. London: Heinemann New Windmill.
Taylor, M.D. (1987). *Roll of Thunder, Hear My Cry*. London: Heinemann New Windmill.

8 The use of literature in the ESL classroom

NAPHEAS AKHTER

My interest and stimulus for wanting to investigate this question arises from my experience of 18 months' teaching ESL (English as a Second Language) from beginner level to GCSE. I have been made aware again and again of the scarcity of resources available in this area, and the often basic and feeble quality of those resources that do exist. Surely there is more to ESL teaching than this?

It is my belief that the time of launching oneself, or being launched, into a language has to be especially stimulating and exciting if interest and progress are to be engendered and maintained. The published materials I have come across are in no way designed to do this. I feel they are more of a hindrance than a guide towards language attainment for the beginner. I am not sure whether it is fear, complacency or inadequacy that is responsible for maintaining this situation.

However, in this chapter, I wish to pursue a very specific line of interest: the effectiveness of the use of authentic literature in the ESL classroom. I mean well-known works of literature, both poetry and prose, as opposed to the mechanical and artificially produced texts tailor-made for ESL students.

> A literary text is authentic text, real language in context, to which we can respond directly. It offers a context in which explanation and discussion of content . . . leads on naturally to examination of language. What is said is bound up very closely with how it is said, and students come to understand and appreciate this.
>
> (Brumfit and Carter, 1987: 15)

When considering the appropriateness of texts to use with foreign students, other factors as well as the authenticity of the text itself have to be taken into consideration. If a teacher is hoping to use a poem, I feel that he or she must ask him/herself certain questions. Does the poem contain a fair representation of the different cultural beliefs within the group of students? Do the feelings, emotions and actions portrayed have a universal applicability or are they peculiar to one culture and thereby not readily understandable by the majority of students? By this I do not mean that the language itself has to be 'universal', but that the emotion contained within it must be readily identifiable by all the students: 'A literary work can transcend both time and culture to speak directly to a reader in another country or a different period of history' (Collie and Slater, 1987: 3).

My ESL class consisted of fifteen students, the majority of whom were aged between 16 and 21 years, though there were also two 'mature' students aged over 35. Three students spoke Vietnamese, two spoke Chinese, two spoke Punjabi, three spoke Bengali, three spoke Urdu and one student was an Afghanistani whose language was Farsi. Three of them had a reasonable command of English; the rest joined the class as beginners.

I chose to look first at a poem called 'Anger' with them. It is a poem written by an 8-year-old girl. At the beginning of the session, I handed out copies of the poem to the students and asked them to read it in silence. When they had finished, I enquired whether there were any words which they did not understand. The language of the poem was quite simple and so we had no major problems with the reading of it:

> I was angry and mad,
> And it seemed that there was hot water inside me,
> And as I got madder and madder.
> The water got hotter and hotter all the time,
> I was in a rage,
> Then I began to see colours,
> Like black and red,
> Then as I got madder and madder,
> My eyes began to pop out of my head,
> They were popping up and down,
> It was horrible,
> And it would not stop,
> I was steaming with anger,
> Nobody could stop me,
> My mother could not stop me,
> Then it was gone,
> And I was all right,
> Horrible, black madness
>
> (Yvonne Lowe aged 8)

Next, I read the poem aloud. The students were split into pairs, ensuring that a stronger student was paired with a weaker one. They were then asked to re-read the poem and note down any opinions, ideas or comments they might have. They were free to discuss these before presenting them to the class. I went round the groups listening to the students and was pleased to hear so much language being used as well as the enthusiasm shown. They all readily identified with the sense of intense anger experienced in the poem.

Some of them recounted occasions when they themselves had been extremely angry and described the physical symptoms of anger they had displayed.

I called the students together and we had a brief discussion of the things that were spoken about in the groups. I asked them if it would be all right for me to tape their responses. They were always rather hesitant, even a little suspicious, when I taped anything, and this occasion was no exception. Nangalay, the Farsi speaker and one of the more able students in the group, volunteered to read the poem and to tell us his feelings about it. We all listened with interest and a few of the students were bold enough to ask him some questions concerning the experiences he had related.

To the weaker students I handed out copies of the poem with some words taken out, a 'cloze' type exercise. Whey they had written their own version of the poem, we matched the words and phrases they had inserted with those in the original poem and discussed how these new words affected the poem and our understanding of it. All of them felt that 'their' words had helped to personalize the poem for them. I felt that this was a positive first step along the road to writing our own poems. One student decided, after some persuasion, that he wanted to recreate dramatically one incident that had caused him great anger. With the help of his classmates he acted out the scene. All of the members of the class watched and commented on the performance. A few others were encouraged to join in as well!

I had enjoyed reading Alice Walker's (1984) poem 'On Sight' and decided that it would be a good idea to share it with the students. We read the poem together and the students spoke of what it had said to each of them. I asked them if they could put down their words in picture form, something very simple but a visual display of what the poem had meant to them. I had drawn a simple picture of the place that I felt Alice Walker to be talking about. After our discussion, I presented my picture to them. This led to a lengthy talk about our favourite places. Everyone contributed by giving an oral description of a special place and explanation of why it was special. They all enjoyed listening to me talking about my college and the friends I had made there who had made the place special for me.

I showed them a picture of Brueghel's 'Icarus' and we read W.H. Auden's poem 'Musée des Beaux Arts'. It was a difficult poem to read, but I felt that it was a continuation of our theme of poems about emotions, as well as an example of a poem being inspired by a visual image. We talked at length about tramps and vagrants, caring and carelessness, homelessness and loneliness. Our session on 'visual' poetry was concluded with a look at an advertisement for a perfume that I felt to be poetical – just a picture, no words at all.

I have always been wary, if not reluctant, when confronted by a long list of words that students want 'meanings' for. It is a scenario that I face with each ESL student to some degree. They hold the belief that each word has a single, set meaning without any variations. Trying to redress this is a difficult and complex business. So we looked at the short poem 'Croft' by Stevie Smith:

Aloft
In the loft
Sits Croft.
He is soft.

This is a poem which fulfils Ezra Pound's criterion of poetry being 'language . . . pared down to its essentials'. I found it to be most effective when illustrating to students the fact that in English one word can have two or more completely different meanings. 'Soft' was the word that we weren't sure about. Did it mean that Croft felt soft to touch or was he 'soft in the head' – stupid, vacant? I wasn't surprised to find that almost all of them knew, or very quickly grasped, the colloquial connotations of the word. They were, none the less, intrigued to find that it could have either meaning or both. By the end of the session, I felt that they had thoroughly mastered the function of the word 'soft' in the poem. This led on nicely to a more detailed study of similar words in the English language. Our study of the poem had enriched our understanding of both the poem and the language.

I also used the poem 'Breakfast' by Jacques Prévert (see Appendix) with students from a weak group. The only words in the poem that I felt I had to explain beforehand were 'café au lait' and 'smoke rings.' We read the poem through in a leisurely manner. Everyone enjoyed it because they could 'read all the words' and they knew what was 'going on' in the poem. We gathered together some props and decided that we would make the poem into a scene from a television programme, maybe even something from *Neighbours* or *East Enders*.

Much enthusiasm was generated and the students, without any help or prompting from me, gave the rest of the group some entertaining performances. What I found interesting was the way in which the more able ones developed certain ideas and incorporated their own interpretations, adding their own dialogue as they went through the actions. I remember particularly a James Bond-ish rendition. The students who could not create their own dialogue went through the actions as the rest of us read the poem aloud chorally. Nobody 'failed': everyone enjoyed a degree of success.

Now that we had explored poetry in some detail and it was no longer a new concept for us, we decided to look around ourselves to find examples of what we considered to be poetry or poetical language. Again the students needed a lot of guidance. I handed out some magazines and left them to read. I asked them to note down examples of any poetic language they came across. Some of their findings included the following:

The husband is like the highlands, the wife is like a spring and the children are flowers and plants. The spring receives and stores the rain from the highlands so that it may give rise to clean streams . . . and cause the flowers, plants and meadows to flourish.

(*Mahjubah*, October 1988)

I chose this magazine because it contained translations in Arabic and Urdu which the students found to be helpful.

We decided to look at some of the examples in detail to see if we could decide why we found them poetical. An advertisement in the *Observer* magazine in November 1988 was deliberately ambiguous:

Take another look at the 190 series –
Mercedes-Benz have.

I showed this to the students because I felt that the work we had already done on words and different levels of meanings would make them appreciate the special point of the final phrase. We compared the advertisement for Heinz Wholesoups:

Increase your pulse-rate and stay healthy

with the Stevie Smith poem. We had some fun with an advertisement for Rover cars:

820e
A 2.0 litre, 16 valve, fuel
injected Rover.
So is the 'e' for expensive?

We set out to discover appropriate 'e' adjectives ourselves, to add to the ones that Rover gave us: 'extravagant, economical, easy'.

I have mentioned already that the students are committed to finding unusual words, writing them down so that they can look them up in the dictionary. Regardless of my own views on the benefits of such an exercise, it is obviously very important to them. Therefore, I needed to find productive ways of incorporating it into my lessons. I chose an advertisement poem containing many words that were unfamiliar to the students:

The Perfect Gentleman

A Gentleman is always discreet.
A Gentleman never lets one down.
A Gentleman is always correct.
A Gentleman is never out of place.
A Gentleman behaves impeccably.
A Gentleman is never showy.
A Gentleman inspires confidence.
A Gentleman embodies taste.
A Gentleman is unmistakable.
A Gentleman has imitators
but no equals.

We read the poem together and made a list of all the difficult words. I altered some of the words so that they would not have difficulty finding them – 'embodies' to 'embody' and 'impeccably' to 'impeccable' – otherwise the dictionaries would have been on their desks for ever. They were asked to put the words into alphabetical order and then to use the dictionary to find the meanings of the words. Their eyes lit up at the prospect and we had a very busy and productive session. We also tried to mould the definition of the words in order to make them apply to the particular poem, giving us a deeper understanding of it. Did they know of any simpler matching words or phrases which could also be used? Then, once the various words and their meanings and connotations had been obtained, the students were split into small groups and asked to talk about the poem. We had a lively report-back session.

I wrote a list of names, each on a separate piece of paper: a woman, a child, a car, a book, a flower, a garden, a ball, a wall and a chair. One piece of paper was given to each group of two students and they were asked to produce a poem similar to 'The Perfect Gentleman'. I could hear and see the students experimenting with words; and not only that, they realized that the language they used 'around' the word had to be modified in order to accommodate the word.

The following poem was written by Amirun and Subera, two girls who are Bengali speakers. They joined the college after spending a short time in Birmingham's Cherrywood induction centre, and both had been in the country for less than 2 years:

A Woman is always working
A Woman never sits down
A Woman laughs like children
A Woman inspires quietness
A Woman can be strong
But she is kind.
I am glad I am a Woman.

This proved a good way for them to see and experience the functions of prepositions, conjunctions, verbs, tenses, and so on. I found it refreshing to witness all this original activity, which stressed again the fact that 'Properly employed you couldn't have a better language and literacy development programme than poetry' (Styles and Triggs, 1988: 4).

Even before I started work on this chapter, I believed that authentic materials could be incorporated successfully into the ESL classroom, no matter how basic the knowledge of the students. The work I have done since to investigate this belief has convinced me even more of the benefits. I have already pointed out the students' enjoyment of the work, but I must not neglect to mention the enjoyment and fulfilment that I myself have gained. After all, teachers need to feel stimulated and motivated by the work they are doing if they are to make it interesting for their students.

So much has been gained by all of us: a greater understanding of ourselves and others within the group, a sense of adventure at reading our first poem, a sense of achievement at writing a poem, the sharing of feelings and ideas as well as the learning of new words, a greater intimacy with the words we already know and their uses. The role of poetry in the language learning process has been made clear to us. As Seamus Heaney wrote:

> For poetry is also essentially about language; it's a form of discourse that strives for precision of the most complex kind . . . a proper encounter with a poem is worth more than weeks of drills and skills and comprehension exercises. It's a language lesson that reveals how language empowers and also how it enslaves.

References

Brumfit, C.J. and Carter, R.A. (1987). *Literature and Language Teaching*. Oxford: Oxford University Press.

Collie, J. and Slater, S. (1987). *Literature in the Language Classroom*. Cambridge: Cambridge University Press.

Ortony, A. (1979). *Metaphor and Thought*. Cambridge: Cambridge University Press.

Styles, M. and Triggs, P. (1988). *Poetry 0–16*. London: Books for Keeps.

Walker, A. (1984). *In Search of our Mothers' Gardens*. London: The Women's Press.

Journals
Language Teaching (January 1989). Cambridge: Cambridge University Press.
Mahjubah (October 1988). Tehran: Foundation of Islamic Thought.

Appendix

Breakfast

He put the coffee
In the cup
He put the milk
In the cup of coffee
He put the sugar
In the café au lait
With the coffee spoon
He stirred
He drank the café au lait
And he set down the cup
Without a word to me
He lit
A cigarette
He made smoke-rings
With the smoke
He put the ashes
In the ash-tray

Without a word to me
Without a look at me
He got up
He put
His hat upon his head
He put his raincoat on
Because it was raining
And he left
In the rain
Without a word
Without a look at me
And I I took
My head in my hand
And I cried.

    Jacques Prevert

Breakfast – a variant

He put the coffee
In the cups
He put the milk
In the cups of coffee
He put the sugar
In the café au lait
With the coffee spoon
He stirred
He drank the café au lait
And he set down the cup
Talking to me
He lit
A cigarette
He made smoke-rings
With the smoke
He put the ashes
In the ash-tray
Talking to me
Looking at me
He got up
His hat upon his head
He put his tee-shirt on
Because it was sunny
And we left
In the sunshine
With a word to me
With a look at me
And I took
My head in my hand
And I laughed.

9 A year 10 story writing project

LENA STRANG

I shall describe here work undertaken with year 10 students that involved writing stories for young children. I do not present this work as a model of what should go in the multiracial classroom, but as an example of what can happen if students are encouraged and motivated enough to have a go.

The class concerned consisted of 22 students, the majority of whom were Asian and whose community languages included Punjabi, Urdu, Bengali and Gujurati. There were also three Afro-Caribbean and two white students. There were certainly opportunities, or so it seemed, to draw on the diversity of experience that existed in the classroom. However, hostility and disaffection on the part of many students and the looming prospect of unemployment around the corner made this difficult. The school was notoriously 'difficult' and the administrative ways of dealing with problems were singularly unhelpful. Work in the classroom was frequently disrupted by absenteeism and spells of suspension. I was concerned about the group and knew that the work they were producing was unimaginative and far below their potential. English work in the school consisted mainly of tedious comprehension-type assignments based on poorly reproduced literature extracts, to be systematically completed for their examination folders.

The ambitious story writing project was largely a desperate response to a difficult situation. Early on in the term, we had read some Asian folk tales which had gone down quite well. I then decided to introduce a Caribbean story which involved group prediction, writing additional scenes in play form and recording individual plays. Carlton and Clive, two of the Afro-Caribbean students who hadn't so far produced any written course work, were keen to act as 'language consultants', and Carlton dictated a sophisticated dialogue in Creole for his partner to write down. An unexpected result of this work was a play written by four Asian pupils which showed remarkable awareness of different language styles. They also managed to record their play in fluent Creole! All the pupils, not just Creole speakers, were able to demonstrate their knowledge of language and their seemingly intuitive ability to make appropriate use of different forms. The plays were displayed on the classroom wall and extracts were printed in the school magazine and the paper published by the local English Centre. I had not quite anticipated the effect this would have on the class. The public acknowledgement of their work seemed to make the effort more worthwhile and they were more prepared to redraft their work now that there was some purpose to it.

I wanted to capitalize on the success of this venture and investigate further the effect writing for a real audience would have. I wanted them to develop into more confident and competent writers and create the contexts where this could take place. With the help of a local storyteller and a member of the city's Multicultural Development Unit with whom I was team teaching, the story writing project was begun.

The purpose of the work was to visit local infant and junior schools and find out, through 'market research', what kind of stories children enjoy. Since they were writing for a specific audience, we hoped they would be able to modify the tasks accordingly and adapt their work in the light of the perceived needs of their 'clients'. By listening to teachers tell stories and by being persuaded to tell stories themselves, we hoped they would become competent storytellers, perhaps as future parents. We wanted to legitimize the use of community languages and encourage them to write bilingual texts. We also hoped to explore and challenge the racial and gender stereotypes inherent in so many traditional children's tales. The end-product – printed storybooks – would at the completion of the project be presented to the children in the junior school classes. The project was to run during one summer term, and a double lesson (lasting 70 minutes) a week was set aside (in fact, when the project did take off, much additional time had to be spent on it).

The initial problem was how to 'sell' the project to the students. There was much resistance at first. The amount of talking and reading involved and the idea of writing for young children did not seem like 'real' work, particularly since the parallel classes were busily filling up their exam folders with literature comprehensions. The fact that they could use this work for assessment provided some reassurance. I don't think we should underestimate the difficulties of changing habitual ways of working, both of students *and* teachers. As the LAPP Project (NFER, 1988: 6) reminds us: 'In practice it has proved hard for many teachers (and indeed pupils) to shift from long-established presuppositions about the kind of attainments that schools value – and related judgements about pupils and what can be expected of them.'

Sense of audience

How, then, did having a real audience affect students' writing? The majority looked forward to the visits to the junior schools. They enjoyed listening and talking to the children and regarded the visits as an essential part of the work. As Malvia said: 'The visits were interesting, I suppose because we saw the kind of stories they enjoyed and their reactions.' The students were able to browse through reading books and observe the children's reactions when teachers told them stories.

Later, the group's thoughts about narrative and what they considered children liked about stories were compiled in list form:

- they like stories to be exciting;
- they like stories with happy endings;
- they can learn about the world outside;
- stories should have a moral at the end;
- they like stories about animals;
- they like stories with cars;
- they like adventure stories;
- pictures make a story more interesting;
- stories can improve their vocabulary.

Through their own experience of narrative and now through conscious exploration, they were able to make explicit their expectations of the genre. In their own writing, they would have to match this expectation.

Abdullah, a student who previously had been difficult to motivate, later developed into a most competent storyteller. Even after two visits to the junior school he was able to observe:

> The voice control [of the teacher telling the story] was good and interested the children and kept them awake . . . The use of hands was very good because people who haven't got much English vocab. will understand the movement of the hands. Making children repeat the words will also make them more interested in the story and will widen their vocabulary.

Many of the students had started drafting their stories even before the first visit. It was interesting to note how willing they were to modify their stories after having met their audience. In some cases, they even started all over again. In the words of Perera (1984), the students had begun 'to learn to think of drafting, revising, editing and proof reading as integral parts of the writing process (essential not just for the novice but for skilled professional writers too)'. They were coming to realize that their first attempt was only a tentative formulation and a way of 'searching for the best expression of their developing meaning' (p. 271).

Pakhan was particularly concerned about the specific needs of his audience: 'I thought about them a lot. I wanted to make sure the children would react in a good way.' He was also unhappy about the ending of his story. In a subsequent recorded evaluation session, he explained how he was helped to resolve the problem (Abdullah was the group leader):

Abdullah: Right, Pakhan what about you?
Pakhan: I had help from other pupils.

Abdullah: In what ways? Can you explain?
Pakhan: Well, they didn't like the ending of my story so . . . I changed it.
Teacher: Do you think it was improved by this?
Pakhan: Yes, it was improved.

Earlier, the students had been inclined to view writing as a private activity, but now they were prepared to share their experiences and 'try out' what they had written on other members of the class.

Pakhan was also influenced by listening to the junior school teacher telling a story about 'The Great Turnip' which involved a great deal of repetition. He noted the rapt attention and active participation of the children as the story unfolded and decided to employ the same techniques in his own story 'How the Giraffe Got His Long Neck'. The story is about a giraffe (with a short neck) who is very curious and has the annoying habit of putting his nose in other people's business. One day, his curiosity gets the better of him and his neck is stuck in a big hole. His friends are persuaded to help him out:

> First the lion tried. He pulled and pulled on the giraffe but still the giraffe was stuck. Then the tiger helped. They both pulled and pulled, but still the giraffe was stuck. Then the monkey helped. They all pulled and pulled and the giraffe's neck became as big as the lion . . . and finally the giraffe's head came out.
>
> (from 'How the Giraffe Got His Long Neck' by Pakhan Singh)

Although the students were clearly influenced by having a specific purpose for their writing, I came to realize that the notion of 'audience' is perhaps not as straightforward as it first appears. Abdullah, helped by Carlton, wrote a very competent story called 'The Ghost Train', which was particularly well received by the children. Surely Abdullah must have had his intended audience clearly in mind when writing his story? His answer is at first rather puzzling:

Teacher: Did you actually have anyone in mind when you were writing it?
Abdullah: No.
Teacher: Because yours had more difficult language in it, did you think about who you were writing for?
Abdullah: No, not really.
Carlton: He just writ it.
Abdullah: I didn't think much about the audience because when you actually read out your story you can change the words according to the ages of the audience.

Although he didn't realize it, Abdullah had very clear ideas of the conventions of writing narrative. He adhered closely to the genre and as he later managed to keep his listeners spellbound when telling them his story, his own expectations of the genre and those of his audience had obviously coincided.

Kress (1982) emphasizes the importance of children learning generic forms as an integral part of the process of learning to write. Smith (1982) also explores the importance of genre and I think his analysis is helpful in explaining what Abdullah and his friends were achieving:

> Effective writing is writing that meets the conventional demands of the text, demands that impose themselves on both writers and readers . . . The text itself – the task at hand – is the primary concern. In other words, between the author and audience is always a specific task, the task of writing an appropriate text in an appropriate register.'

> (Smith, 1982: 4)

Some of the stories are original like 'The Ghost Train' (although Abdullah acknowledges his indebtness to C.S. Lewis!); others are adaptations of traditional stories. There was a version of 'Billy and the Beanstalk' and two different versions of 'Goldilocks and the Three Bears'. I do not think this in any way detracts from the achievements of the students. They had still internalized the genres and were able to apply their knowledge in their own writing.

Combating stereotypes

We wanted the students to be aware of traditional stereotypes in stories which often have white middle-class bias. We noted the omission of Asian and black characters and the portrayal of girls in submissive roles. In discussions, the students pointed out that they themselves had grown up on this diet. There was some familiarity with traditional Asian stories and we were able to identify elements common to folk tales. It was inevitable that the students' choices for stories were informed by their own reading, but there were several attempts at dealing with both racial and gender stereotyping.

Rita and Arfah decided to write a story about 'Jack and the Princess'. While Jack, a traditional miller's son, wins the hand of his beloved, the princess in this case is a dark-haired Indian girl dressed in a beautiful sari. One way of trying to redress bias! One of the main characters in 'The Ghost Train' is white, whereas the other is black. Strong female characters feature in both versions of 'Goldilocks and the Three Bears'. In one story, the bears are terrorized by Goldilocks but they are all in the end outwitted by Red Riding Hood. In the second version, Goldilocks is really Supergirl in disguise, and in dealing with the greedy bears is aided by the resourceful Supergran! These two stories remained firm favourites with the children.

Use of home languages

We tried to validate the use of home languages in the classroom and encourage the students to use these when telling and writing stories. A sixth-form student was invited to tell the class stories in Urdu and the support teacher involved in the project told stories in Gujurati. During their first visit to the junior school, two students volunteered to tell stories in Urdu while one of the children reciprocated by telling a story in Gujurati using a cardboard cut-out of a greedy cat!

We realized that the students' competence in their home languages varied enormously. Some felt confident enough to tell stories, whereas others lacked the necessary fluency. However, at the end of the summer term, a group of children were invited to the school and, with the help of the Media Studies Department, a storytelling session with students using their home languages was video-taped.

Some of the students had basic literacy in Urdu, but calligraphy had to be done by hand (since printing in Urdu was not available at the time) and this placed too many obstacles in the way. After the completion of the books, two were translated into Urdu by a sixth-form student who also managed to undertake the calligraphy. Translations into Punjabi and Bengali by sixth-form students were made easier by access to printing facilities in the city. We realized, however, that there is a need for books printed in home languages in the junior school classroom and our modest attempts were welcomed. As the DES (1984) report on mother-tongue provision points out:

> A greater problem for certain languages is the availability of materials of qual-
> ity appropriate to the needs of the pupils. This problem, where it exists, is
> compounded by teachers' uncertainty about what is available in this country
> and how to acquire stocks.
>
> (*Times Educational Supplement*, 31 January 1986)

Uma Ram Nath surveys the field of mother-tongue materials and observes that there is a dearth of commercially produced material. Most of the texts available have been produced through voluntary initiatives and while laudable tend to lack finish and gloss. While Uma Ram Nath applauds the initiative, he concludes: 'This is sad because very often children have a deep seated need for mother tongue publications, of whichever quality, and the teaching apparatus is not geared to fulfilling it' (p. 37).

I also think it was important for the young children to see older students from their own communities in status roles and for the languages to be used for real educational purposes.

The process

Did the project help the students to develop into more confident and competent writers? I would say yes. Their attitude towards writing underwent a marked change. Before they would have been reluctant to modify any piece of work and regarded writing as a once-and-for-all activity. Now drafting was seen to be a necessity and part of the process of writing stories.

Collaboration increased throughout the project. This was particularly true when they were faced with the apparently mammoth task of illustrating their stories. There were long queues by Christian's desk – he was an excellent artist after all! Taking advantage of various expertise in the class seemed the obvious thing to do.

In the last hectic days, as the deadline approached, the classroom turned into a workshop where different activities were being undertaken – typing up stories, designing covers, letra-setting titles and numbering pages using dry letter transfers. Even the stray student wandering in the corridor was attracted by the buzzing atmosphere in the classroom and offered his assistance! Perhaps this approximates to what Orme (1983) terms 'the workshop approach', where attempts are made to create writing situations which resemble the ones 'real' writers have to work in. However, he acknowledges the slight problems involved in running an English workshop: 'not least explaining the levels of noise and physical activity that takes place in what was once a quiet and studious classroom – duplicators being turned, typewriters clattering and editorial committees in session!' (p. 35).

Against all odds, the books were ready to be presented to the junior school children in the last week of term. The students took obvious pleasure in seeing their own work in print and having an appreciative audience listening to the authors telling their own stories. In a radio programme later made about the project, Abdullah captured this feeling:

> I've learnt what children like out of a story . . . I've learnt it's not as easy as it looks; it's a lengthy process . . . but when the actual book is finished, it's great to see your book lying there and the children enjoying it. That's the greatest part of all – the children enjoying the stories.

The students were involved in the whole process of book production – from the first inception of the story to binding the final typed version. I think this did much to demystify both the writing and publishing of books and for the students to see themselves as authors. Pakhan assesses what the project meant to him: 'I enjoyed actually planning the books, binding them, drawing the pictures for them . . . really the total process.'

Being assured that there is a huge demand for books like these in junior schools, we decided to market them commercially – at affordable prices. Publicity material was designed and sent out to schools and books were printed in bulk at the school's Project Centre. Students in other subject areas were now drawn into production as book orders poured in.

The second stage of the project was characterized by the students becoming involved in dissemination of what they had learnt. Groups of students took part in television and radio programmes and participated in numerous teacher workshops and conferences. One of the radio commentators observed the ease with which the students were now interacting with children: 'The students have obviously learnt a wide range of skills and it was very impressive to see them relating to a whole class with the confidence of professional teachers.'

It is difficult to ascertain the direct results of the work. However, it was particularly gratifying to see the achievements of 'non-exam' students, who had previously been 'written off' by the school. It appears as if the build-up of confidence and self-esteem transferred themselves to other subject areas and certainly attendance improved markedly. An added corollary was to see the increased motivation of boys in a part of the curriculum where traditionally girls tend to be greater achievers.

Finally, the partnership with the junior schools was mutually beneficial. The older students were involved with the younger ones in real learning situations. The close interconnection between reading and writing may have become more apparent to the younger children, and perhaps they may have been helped as developing readers and writers themselves.

Conclusion

The book writing project demonstrates what can be achieved in the classroom if the notion of students as merely passive consumers of knowledge deemed superior to their own is rejected. The arena of education has always been a battleground and where advances have been made, backlashes soon follow. The blurb for a book published not very long ago (Marenbon, 1987) makes interesting reading in this context:

> A 'new orthodoxy' in English teaching is sweeping away many of the traditional landmarks; replacing concepts of accuracy with those of appropriateness; proclaiming the doctrine of linguistic equality; preaching the virtues of 'oracy' and the relegation of grammar; and neglecting our literary heritage in favour of encouraging 'pupil response'.

As a teacher concerned with the achievement of students in the multiracial classroom, I would want to safeguard much of this 'new orthodoxy'.

References

Department of Education and Science (1984). *Mother Tongue Teaching in School and Community*. HMI Inquiry in four LEAs. London: HMSO.

Kress, G. (1982). *Learning to Write*. London: Routledge and Kegan Paul.

Marenbon, J. (1987). *English our English*. London: Centre for Policy Studies.

Nath, U.R. (1986). Four corners: In search of multicultural materials. *The Times Educational Supplement*, 31 January.

National Foundation for Educational Research (1988). *Lower Attaining Pupils' Programme. The Search for Success – An Overview of the Programme*. London: NFER.

Orme, D. (1983). The workshop approach. *The Times Educational Supplement*, 25 November.

Perera, K. (1984). *Children's Writing and Reading: Analysing Classroom Language*. Oxford: Basil Blackwell.

Smith, F. (1982). *Writing and the Writer*. London: Heinemann Educational.

10 Widening the field: New literature for older students

EMRYS EVANS

The Cox Report's welcome insistence, for England and Wales, on the place of literature written in English but not in England (DES, 1989; this volume, p. 2), makes room for a wealth of myth, folklore, poetry, children's literature and other material for children up to the age of 16. The National Council for the Teaching of English (NCTE) has also shown a proper concern for the use of similar material in the USA by devoting part of a special issue of its *English Journal* (NCTE, 1990) to the question.

For older students, especially those in the 16–19 age range, there are many novels, poems and plays which can be introduced under the same rubric. Until recently, in the UK in particular, but also in some Australian states and elsewhere, the study of literature at this level has been narrowed by the emphasis on 'close study' of a very few examination texts. The value of such close study is certainly considerable, but not if it is allowed to take over examination syllabuses and school curricula to the exclusion of wider reading. Benton and Fox's (1985) progressive hierarchy of reading – meeting, then sharing, then studying – is best catered for when young people can *meet* ('be introduced to') a wide variety of literature, *share* some with each other and their teacher, and *study* in depth only a small proportion of what they meet and share.

When work in literature for 16- to 19-year-olds is largely dominated by examination syllabuses, recent changes have made available a larger proportion of assessment based on course work, and with it a much greater opportunity for schools and colleges – even for individual teachers and students – to choose their own texts. Nor surprisingly, in inner-city areas in England and Wales, where the proportion of children from Indian, Pakistani, Bangladeshi and Caribbean families has increased considerably in recent years, this freedom has led to the choice of writers like V.S. Naipaul, R.K. Narayan, Ruth Prawer Jhabvala, Anita Desai, Samuel Selvon and others, as appropriate material for study. On the other hand, it is probably true that in schools in those areas of the country least affected by the arrival of families from overseas and their descendants, British and American literature have tended to form the majority, and often the whole, of the choice made. The case study in this chapter describes the writer's introduction of a selection of other 'overseas English literature' into such a school. It was also my personal aim in offering this course that the students should have the chance to share the enjoyment I have found in the following six novels:

From South Africa: Andre Brink, *A Dry White Season*
                      J.M. Coetzee, *The Life and Times of Michael K*
From India: Ruth Prawer Jhabvala, *The Householder*
From the USA: Toni Morrison, *Beloved*
From the Caribbean: V.S. Naipaul, *Miguel Street*
From East Africa: Ngũgĩ wa Thiong'o, *The River Between*

There were twelve students in the group, six boys and six girls. We worked together for just over an hour every Tuesday afternoon for 10 weeks, with a final eleventh session a couple of weeks after the tenth, and a gap of 3 weeks in the middle for a half-term holiday and some examinations. In the first three or four sessions, we discussed the purpose of the work. To begin with, I took in a box containing three copies of each of my six novels. I introduced the books and invited the students to choose from among them. We talked about the widening scope of English-language literature outside Britain, and considered some of the approaches to reading they might find useful. We explicitly discussed Benton and Fox's 'meeting, sharing, studying' hierarchy and, as the term went on, we saw ourselves at different times as meeting, sharing or studying our texts.

In the second session, I asked them to spend 20 minutes recording their first impressions of the novel they had chosen, and we discussed headings they might use in their reading journals, like background, places, relationships, language, form, things that surprised them as readers, or delighted them, or puzzled them. The third time we met we exchanged brief reports on what they had been reading. Some referred to journal notes; some expressed themselves sufficiently interested to want to read more in their first choices; some wanted to change their books. I suggested ways they could begin to consider planning an assignment for the term: they might take two or three related works by different authors; they might aim to become the local authority on one particular novelist; or they might prefer to concentrate on one country, or on a common theme in more than one writer's work.

By the fifth session, with the 3-week break approaching, first ideas for written work were being proposed. The students suggested the titles themselves and we discussed them. In most cases, a choice of a central text had been made. So far, we had had a number of reactions to my six books. Andre Brink appealed to several students. Jo made a comparison between Brink's approach to the dilemmas of his society in *A Dry White Season*, which has a contemporary setting, and the historical setting of his *An Instant in the Wind*, while Kate B bridged a wide gap of cultures by attempting to contrast the styles of Brink and Jhabvala.

Coetzee's writing, as I had expected, put some people off, while others got hooked on it. Phil chose to look at the sidelong way the author builds up the central character and the political metaphor in *Life and Times of Michael K*. Simon G (there were three Simons among the six boys!), having read *Michael K* and *A Dry White Season*, borrowed another novel by Coetzee, *Waiting for the Barbarians*. His assignment, based on this novel, was the only one to take up the possibility I had offered of attempting what Peter Adams calls 'dependent authorship' (Corcoran and Evans, 1987: ch. 6). He wrote an alternative ending to Coetzee's story. To do this, he had to cope with several problems of the novelist's sophisticated style – his consistent use of the present tense, the brevity of many of his sentences, and the continually crippling self-consciousness of the central character, the old magistrate. He did not, I think, clearly understand all of these constraints, but his piece showed great depth of sympathy with the novel, and seemed to me at least as significant an achievement as a sound piece of critical prose would have been.

I had expected Ngũgĩ to be the remotest of the six authors from the experience of these sixth formers. However, the remoteness seemed to be a positive attraction. Three of the students chose to write on Ngũgĩ. Matthew's was not a very successful piece, but the other two were among the most accomplished of the group. Simon F, who said relatively little in our class discussions, chose to look at the influence of the white man in *The River Between*. Since no white man actually appears in the story – as opposed, say, to Chinua Achebe's *Things Fall Apart*, or other novels by Ngũgĩ himself – this was an interesting and challenging topic. Simon studied it very effectively, in terms both of indirect influence on Kikuyu concepts of religion, education and politics, and also of Ngũgĩ's deliberate choice to maintain only a shadowy sense of the early white presence in colonial Kenya. In the last paragraph of his assignment, Simon sums up what he sees as Ngũgĩ's viewpoint – that of his main character, the young teacher Waiyaki – and his objectives in his novel:

Throughout *The River Between*, Ngũgĩ works from Waiyaki's point of view – that is, of a young man attempting to deal with a tribal split caused by fear of the unknown white man. It may be this native 'innocence' of the white [*sic*] that Ngũgĩ is perhaps attempting to represent in his writing – that is, maintaining a mystery about the whites so that his reader may experience an amount of the unknown that the tribes encountered. Ngũgĩ can also be seen to deal more with the effect rather than with the cause. As with Waiyaki's schooling, Joshua's Christian beliefs and the general situation of the whites in the black community – Ngũgĩ only deals with the events affected by the white influence on the tribal communities. And consequent to this, we are led to see that Ngũgĩ lays no judgement on the white beliefs and attitudes, but criticises more the blacks' response, and ultimate division, to the whites.

As I commented on the assignment, 'here and there the complexity of the argument defeats the clarity of your prose style', but here is a young writer genuinely attempting to grapple with a situation he has found interesting and challenging.

Rachael, who had read *The River Between* with evident interest and then borrowed two other books by Ngũgĩ, wrote a comparison between the two early novels, *The River Between* and *Weep Not, Child*. As we shall see, she then went on to develop this work in her extended essay.

Jhabvala's *The Householder* was not a great success with this group, though I have heard that students in other schools have enjoyed it much more. Three people borrowed copies, but I suspect only one actually finished it – Kate B, who wrote about it along with Brink's *A Dry White Season*. Vic, however, remembered that the same author had also written both the novel and the filmscript *Heat and Dust*, and wrote an interesting comparison between the film and the novel.

Several students borrowed *Beloved* – perhaps the 'biggest' of the texts offered – and read part or all of it. What I could not have foreseen in the case of Kate was that, having missed my first session with the group because she was still involved in a school exchange visit to Georgia, USA, she would then take up *Beloved*, and through it Morrison's other work, with special enthusiasm. Her coursework assignment was a comparison between *Beloved* and *Tar Baby* as far as each deals with slavery, literal or metaphorical. But she was the second of the two students who went on to take their extended essay topics from our work. Not surprisingly, she herself attributed her initial interest in Morrison to her own American experience.

After the 3-week break for half-term and the exams, we only had four official weeks left. Getting the assignments written, in draft and then in their final versions, had become the predominant concern. I was working with individual students most of the time, except when I discussed general points about writing or read them an occasional short story. But I was able to use one of these sessions for what was, for many of us, a high point of the course.

Constance Ovonji, from Uganda, who was studying for her master's degree at Birmingham that year, agreed to come and spend an hour with us. She brought with her some photocopied excerpts from the Ugandan poet Okot p'Bitek's *Song of Lawino*, which we read together and talked about. She told us something of the tribal groups she and Okot belonged to, and the related languages they spoke. She also talked about her own experiences; for example, how during her 3 years' undergraduate study at Makerere University there had never been any running water on campus, and what it was like to live in a city where a single night *without* the sound of gunfire was a phenomenon that needed explaining! In doing all this, she brought into the classroom the lively and intelligent presence of a person of different culture, race, nationality and upbringing from any of us who had been working together. How far such encounters are essential to work of this kind it would be difficult to judge, but their value, when they can be arranged, is considerable.

Two additional lists go with this chapter. The first is of a few short stories I read aloud to supplement the six novels, by a black South African author and by two Indian-born English-language novelists, and for teachers, details of some books I have referred to and others which might be useful (see pp. 152–3).

The second list is of additional books which were read by individual students, either during the course and for their coursework assignments or, in the cases of Kate F and Rachael, for their extended essays. I think perhaps this list is one of the chief successes of the course: a number of eyes and minds were opened to a range of literature they might not otherwise have met. Things the students said, and notes and letters I had from them at and after the end of the course, suggested a lively and genuine interest.

As to the extended essays, this was an entirely personal choice. Every student had to write an essay of about 3000 words for the exam. The selection of topics and the devising of a title was their responsibility, so long as it was a literary topic, but the work would be supervised by a teacher. I offered to supervise any topics related to my course. The process went on, for the two students who chose to work with me, for nearly a year after the end of the formal course. We met about once a month when school was in session, and in the meantime both students sent me outlines of their intentions, drafts of chapters and sections they were working on, and letters explaining what they were doing (and just occasionally what they *weren't* doing, and why!).

The results were two very good essays. Rachael, who had written earlier on two novels by Ngũgĩ, went on to compare them with the three by Chinua Achebe which have been brought together as his 'African Trilogy'. In particular, she considered Achebe's presentation of the Igbos of Eastern Nigeria – a 'self-sufficient, positive, secure, balanced society', as she saw it – in *Things Fall Apart*, and Ngũgĩ's of the Kikuyu tribes, held together by the ceremonies of circumcision, in *The River Between*. She studied the ways conflict was introduced into each of these societies, both from inside, as between the villages of Umuofia, and from outside, especially through the intervention of white administrators and missionaries. She compared the personalities of the distant Livingstone in Ngũgĩ and such contrasting characters as the missionaries Brown and Smith in Achebe. Often she found appropriate references to support her argument, as for example, in looking at the zealous Reverend James Smith: 'there was a saying in Umuofia that as a man danced so the drums were beaten for him. Mr Smith danced a furious step and so the drums went mad.'

Kate's initial enthusiasm for *Beloved* led her to read eventually all Toni Morrison's novels so far published. To give her own writing shape, she chose three particular points to consider: Morrison's presentation of the relationships between different groups of people, her concern with her characters' sense of their own identity, and the style and structure of her novels. Among the relationships she distinguished were those between parents and children, betwen black and white people, and between men and women. The parent–child relationships demanded consideration of some of the extremes of behaviour Morrison shows us: child abuse by a father in *The Bluest Eye* and perversions of mother love in *Tar Baby* and *Song of Solomon*. An interesting passage pursued the course of Milkman's search for his identity, disabled by his nickname and yet, in Kate's view, achieving a sense of himself more successfully than any of Morrison's other characters. In all this, great poise and maturity were required and demonstrated by this upper secondary school student. Finally, in discussing the structure and style of Morrison's novels, Kate isolated her use of 'people's thought processes', as in her presentation of Pecola's schizophrenic mind talking to itself in *The Bluest Eye*, or in the mutual recognition of mother and daughter towards the end of *Beloved*: 'a beautiful passage, but menacing – the emotions are far too strong to be anything but dangerous, and both know this'.

For these students, their encounter with English literature of the kind Cox recommends was at least an interesting experience. Possibly the fact that the sessions were led by an outsider made it even more unusual for them, but of course that is by no means necessary or desirable. For the two who wrote extended essays, it was clearly a very special reading experience, and their personal letters to me made it quite clear that each was relating her African and American reading very clearly to elements in her own personal life. Other members of the group showed in their contributions to our talk in class and in their assignments that they were willing and able to take the new opportunity seriously and constructively. Perhaps there were one or two who did not make the most of it: surely there always would be!

The widening of cultural experience, through reading, of members of the majority in any society is vitally important. It needs, of course, to start before the sixth form or its grade 12 or 13 equivalent. But at that level, the richness of the field to be explored, in poetry, drama and non-fictional prose, as well as in novels, invites teachers to new and very rewarding work.

References

Benton, M. and Fox, G. (1985). *Teaching Literature Nine to Fourteen*. Oxford: Oxford University Press.

Corcoran, B. and Evans, E. (1987). *Readers, Texts, Teachers*. Milton Keynes: Open University Press.

Department of Education and Science (1989). *English for Ages 5 to 16* (The Cox Report). London: DES and the Welsh Office.

National Council for the Teaching of English (1990). A global perspective. *The English Journal*, 79(8), December: 16–28.

11 Bringing the writer in from the cold

JIM KABLE

In early 1982, the Sydney writer Angelo Loukakis addressed a seminar of those teaching English as a Second Language (ESL) on the issue of using real writing (not bowdlerized or structured) which was Australian as a focus for their students. His thoughts gave validity to the very practices I was pursuing with my students (see Chapter 4). Because he was a writer, and the first I had ever met, I took very much to heart the message he had for me as a teacher of recently arrived immigrant children. There was more. He also broadened considerably my understanding of what constituted Australian writing. Traditionally, this term conjured up visions of nineteenth-century male figures and a few early twentieth-century female writers, and it was very Anglo-centric. He redefined it as 'anything written in English in the way of prose or poetry by any person who cares to call themselves Australian, whether they are in residence or expatriated'. Although I have since altered this definition for myself, to encompass a wider range of writing and writers, it was a valuable shift of emphasis for me at the time. This picture was supported by Angelo Loukakis' reference to two pieces of writing which he paralleled as quintessentially Australian. George Johnston's *My Brother Jack* takes the reader through the Australia encompassed by both World Wars. The other novel, *Flying Home*, by Morris Lurie, also a Melbourne writer, is a tale which in its most significant part chronicles the very Australian theme of finding one's ancestral roots and, in so doing, understanding one's own particular existence.

During a period spent out of the classroom, I was able to consider my teaching, to uncover some of the threads and unravel the basis of the patterns which seemed to draw my students into successful learning. I tested some of my ideas in the field as a guest teacher over a 10-week period with a senior class. There were 15 students representing cultural and linguistic backgrounds as widely diverse as Arabic (both Christian and Muslim Lebanese), Greek (from Greece and Cyprus), Indonesian, Italian (and several years living in French-speaking New Caledonia), Serbian, Spanish-speaking from South America (including one young man whose family had earlier emigrated to Venezuela from Syria) and Vietnamese. Although they were fortunate in having a teacher who was concerned both professionally and personally in their educational progress, it is fair to suggest that they were in many cases the victims of a system which excluded them from mainstream English teaching, leading some of them to see themselves as inadequate or as failures in their English studies. One boy had in fact 'switched off' almost entirely. I discovered that he had been in Australia since year 4 in primary school. Seven years later, he was still in a specialist ESL class. Who could blame him for his lack of involvement?

Apart from my reasons for being with them and the actual mechanics involved in getting to know each other as well as to study some Australian writing together, I also, importantly, wanted to 'introduce' them to the writers whose works I had chosen. In order to help them make connections, I did my best to select authors who were either from the same cultural or linguistic background as the students or who reflected aspects of it in some way within the story or poem. I brought along copies of their published works, passed around photos if I had any, or told personal-interest stories to which I was privy about the writers. During my time with the students, I usually set some writing activity to be completed by the next lesson. But it was the final written exercise which produced the best results, and something which I am sure they will never forget. All the pieces selected were by contemporary authors and so I asked the students to choose their favourite piece and to write a letter to the author. In response came lovely letters and even copies of books from all but one author. The following four pieces were my students' favourites.

Gail Hennessy's poem 'Mondays' contains the lines:

My Irish Grand-mother said:
'There's a proper way
even to hanging out
washing.'

This led us into a wide-ranging discussion and exploration of cultural differences and the variety of 'proper ways' our different cultures suggest.

Spiro Zavos' story 'Tales out of School' examines the experiences of a schoolboy who is culturally different from the rest and the misunderstandings which arise. Seen through the eyes of the boy, his teacher and a classmate, the reader becomes aware of different ways of perception. The mispronunciation of the boy's name rang true in the experience of many class members.

Andras Dezsery, pioneer multilingual publisher and writer, had written a story entitled 'A Handful of Earth from Home', which deals with the theme of homesickness and adjustment to the new landscape. Reference to the character's Hungarian room, decorated so as to stave off the alienation of the new land, allowed the class to talk about similar ornaments and objects at home which were connections with their own countries of origin and demonstrated aspects of their cultures.

Mena Abdullah and Ray Mathew's story 'Grandfather Tiger' draws on the Punjabi background (both Hindu and Muslim) of a little girl beginning school in Australia who is advised to wear her own name and her own clothes so that she may be better understood by her fellows.

In my next job, I was involved in teaching adult community classes. One class, consisting entirely of elderly Jewish Russians, I was to meet first of all in a visiting capacity. Determined to make the most of our meeting, I took along with me a story by my favourite Australian writer, Judah Waten. I knew that his background, while politically of the left, was Jewish, and thought that it was this connection I might emphasize. Born in Odessa in 1911, and having spent a brief time in Palestine, he arrived as a toddler in Western Australia early in 1914. I held up his autobiographical *From Odessa to Odessa* while adding that he lived then in Melbourne and had a daughter playing violin in the Sydney Symphony Orchestra. The murmur from the crowded classroom rose because, as I discovered, most of them had been born in Odessa, too. How fortuitous! I explained that he had been one of the first Australian writers to deal explicitly with aspects of cultural differences in this country. I then read aloud from his brief autobiographical story, 'Born in Odessa' (in Waten, 1978).

In this story, Judah Waten illustrates the emphasis placed in his childhood home on both music and literature. His mother had sighted Chekhov entering the Odessa Hotel from the Maritime Parade. She had met Hayim Nachman Bialik and actually listened to Mendele Mechor Sforim and Sholem Aleichem reading from their writing. When I attempted to pronounce these names and to say in Yiddish the names of two songs referred to ('Oifyn boidem shloft der dach' and 'Yiddel mit dem fiddel, Berel mit dem bass'), everyone joined in, *en masse*. Adult learners need to be treated as adults by being challenged in their learning with materials permitting them to draw directly upon their accumulated experiences of life, including their reading.

As I was to discover when I returned later on a regular basis with some members of this group – who were highly educated, cultured and widely read – Australian writer Dymphna Cusack was a favourite back in the Soviet Union. I found myself reading her 1955 novel, *The Sun in Exile*, in which a young Australian artist in London meets and marries an African. Cusack analyses the prejudice faced directly and indirectly by the couple. It was more than reassuring to find that this novel did not end in the kind of tragedy often used in the past to morally underline the futility or foolhardiness of such relationships. I was left with the sense of a couple who would blaze trails for a new order of justice and equality.

With another group with whom I pursued a programme of short

Australian writing (stories and poems reflective of immigrant experience and cultural and linguistic differences), I began to invite writers to the classroom. Our first visitor was Linda Burney, then the Executive Officer of the State Aboriginal (Koori) Education Consultative Group. Although more of a curriculum writer, she knew of the power of Koori writers to encourage educationally disaffected Koori teenagers, including Koori playwright Robert Merritt's *The Cakeman*. She spent an illuminating hour providing a Koori perspective to Australian history, a perspective which up until recent times had been largely denied or ignored. Her words were a fine introduction to our examination of poems by writer Jack Davis, poet and playwright of the Bibbulmum peoples of south-western Western Australia.

Olga Masters responded to an invitation by reading to us a story from her work in progress, *A Long Time Dying*. She told us of her work and past experiences and quoted to us from an unknown Chinese poet to describe why she did her writing in the very early morning: 'Now that I am old I wake early in the morning And feel like God Who has created the world.' One student arrived with a copy of one of her earlier books, *The Home Girls*, duly signed by Olga Masters, while the following week another member of the class brought along a newspaper clipping about Ms Masters.

When Pino Bosi came to visit, his wide-ranging discussion of literature and of life and of language, all liberally sprinkled with the names of writers from a range of cultures, there were several people in the class who discovered for the first time that one of their favourite writers (in Spanish) was an Australian, Morris West. Pino Bosi was 18 when he first arrived in Australia. A fluent speaker of formal standard English, he knew nothing of the mysteries of colloquial usage, especially its Australian forms. He believes that he really only began to understand all of the subtle allusions and nuances of English as he read and learnt the range of English nursery rhymes when his children came along and went to school. Six members of the class purchased a copy of his collection of short stories, *Checkmate*, and our study of one of the stories redefined the sense of alienation and of belonging as it contrasted the land where one was born with that sacred soil within which one was buried.

Poet and writer Peter Skrzynecki impressed the class with his quiet sincerity. He outlined the milestones in his life since he had arrived in Australia aged 4 years in 1949. Educated in Sydney, he began his teaching career with several very important years in one-teacher schools in 'the bush'. Touching on his contemporary literary life drew in many of the Chinese students who recognized the names he mentioned. And the following week, not only was there a poem from Peter Skrzynecki, but there was also an article about Pino Bosi and his family at home in the nationwide newspaper, *The Australian*. We read these together in class, a literary and journalistic recognition of 'our' writers.

The final phase in my concern for Australian writers with roots in other cultures developed in my last home teaching position. In that post I emphasized the importance of writers to an understanding of their work, as well as the enormous satisfaction which comes to the students from being in contact either by letter or in person with the writers themselves. Since early 1986, I have been living and teaching in a small coastal resort centred around Nelson Bay, several hundred kilometres north of Sydney. I had suffered a degree of marginalization at state and national English teaching conferences where I felt that, although my experiences showed the way as much for teachers of mainstream English as for teachers of ESL, the promotion of my workshop sessions seemed to suggest relevance only for the latter. I have since had the opportunity to confirm that Australian writing that focuses on the nation's cultural diversity is indeed as useful for native speakers of English as for those of non-English-speaking ethnic origins, all of whom are interested in seeing reflections of their own cultural traditions as well as learning the other elements which together constitute the rich fabric of Australian society. And it is in this reading and consideration that they are able to expand on their insights and on the perceptions raised in the literature being studied.

Several students in my first year in this new school wrote to writers whose works had personally appealed to them in one way or another. The immediate appeal for Robert in John J. Encarnação's 'Football Like She is Played' was that Robert himself was the best and fairest in the local competition. But when the reply came back, it was to let Robert know that upon arrival from East Timor during the Second World War, Encarnação had actually lived for a time in a refugee camp set up at Bob's Farm, which was now Robert's address. Lois wrote to Hanna Foks about her ironic autobiographical piece 'Ambitions, Illusions and Facts'. Lois had an Italian brother-in-law and had pursued ballet for quite a number of years. The letter written by Lois became Hanna's second piece of fanmail. She had known Egon E. Kisch in Paris in the 1930s, both before and after his controversial visit to Australia, when he came to warn of the dangers presented by the Nazis in Germany. Peter Skrzynecki suggested to Garrin that part of a writer's artistic vision comes from confronting a different landscape, as he had found when he left Sydney to teach in small rural communities. The contrast had given rise to an urge to communicate his fascination in written forms. Children's writer Margaret Sharpe told the story of a little Aranda girl from Alice Springs. In *The Traeger Kid*, the reader follows her activities and concerns at school, visiting the camp in the family's homeland, going on a visit to relatives living in Brisbane and attending a relative's funeral in northern New South Wales. It gently uncovers a lot about Koori culture and languages, and when my junior students wrote to her she not only wrote back individual letters but came to visit, explaining how her professional career as a sociolinguist, particularly among Koori peoples, had enabled her and motivated her to write this story. She explained that because she was not Koori herself, she had not presumed to be able to think for her principal character, and so the story is essentially one of external observation, with no inner thoughts. The school principal made a special grant which enabled us to purchase a set of the books.

In some ways, this has been the most truly satisfying link of all, for I have been able to show that writers are not people who lived in other times or in other places. There are many writers in every community, of course, and my own is no different. Local poet Iris Fisher visited one of my classes and told of the early alienation and homesickness she had felt after emigrating from England and how this had become the impetus of her writing, despite limited education as a girl. We listened to her very first poem, 'Letter to England', in which she examined that homesickness. Daphne Rooke, originally from South Africa, where she knew Alan Paton and where several of her books had been banned, and who had set several children's books, including *Double Ex*, in the Nelson Bay locale, dealing with post-war refugees who were initially housed in a camp here, came along to talk about her writing. Joanna Lafebre, originally invited along to address some of the issues of being an immigrant with one of my history classes, returned to speak to a final year English class involved in examining the cultural diversity of Australian society, the focus being the volume *Joseph's Coat*, edited by Peter Skrzynecki. But she came with a profoundly moving piece of prose she had just written, called 'Rugged Times'. She returned again to read to a different class another story also set during the time in which the Netherlands was occupied by the Nazis, 'A Minor Incident'. We were learning something of the special courage and resilience of spirit brought to Australia by the many 'ordinary' people who have arrived as immigrants and refugees.

Peter Skrzynecki, as editor of *Joseph's Coat* and one of the writers studied, came to speak to the year 12 class studying his book. From six of the other writers whose works we were to study came letters and even, in one case, a documentary video, speaking directly to my class about themselves, about the inspiration for their writing and about their understanding of our society. These writers, generous and concerned for my isolated students, included Alma Aldrete (originally from Spanish-speaking Texas), Margaret Diesendorf (an escapee from the horrors of Nazi-occupied Austria), Lolo Houbein (who grew up in the war-wasted Netherlands and who underscores the irony of those who fight for peace), Ania Walwicz (from Poland, whose poetic style draws the reader into its flow and causes us to see from other points of view), Spiro Zavos (from New Zealand) and Yota Krili-Kevans (who arrived as a young woman from Greece and graduated from factory work and university, giving her particular insights into our society). My year 12 students responded with their own *True Stories – Year 12 Remembers*, about which more has been written elsewhere, answering the issues and experiences from *Joseph's Coat* with their own.

Other writers who have responded to student letters include Ruth Park, the New Zealand-born author of the time-shift novel *Playing Beatie Bow*, with its Orkney characters and patterns of speech; Nadia Wheatley, whose *Five Times Dizzy* tells the contemporary story of a little girl called Mareka whose Greek immigrant parents own a shop in inner-city Sydney. How she deals with the arrival of her elderly Yaya (grandmother) and the resolution of her conflict with her Anglo-Australian playmates is not only an enjoyable adventure but it explodes lots of stereotypes. Nadia Wheatley has spent a lot of time in Greece, especially in Crete, and was a close friend of Martin Johnston, one of the children of the writers George Johnston and Charmian Clift, who grew up on the Greek Island of Hydra. Barbara Ker Wilson, English-born writer and editor and author of *Jane Austen in Australia*, not only wrote but also came to visit as well, bringing alive the middle-class world of Jane Austen's England in a way that made her novels accessible to my students.

And most recently, Gillian Bouras, author of a text I have been studying with another year 12 group, was persuaded to come and speak directly to my class while in Australia visiting her family. *A Foreign Wife* tells of the cultural adjustments she had to make when in 1980 she moved from Melbourne to a village in the Greek Peloponnese with her Greek-born husband and two small children. Her book explains the immigrant experience from an Anglo-Australian perspective and it is immediately accessible for English-speaking Australians, as well as being recognizable by those of other immigrant origins here. Her visit confirmed the understanding of my students.

Tell your students those things about the writers you are studying which illustrate why their concerns can be trusted. And the things which make them interesting human beings anyway. Above all else, the writers must come alive as real people and the best way to do this is to bring the writers into your classroom. Have your students write letters. Invite the writers to visit. Bring them in out of the cold.

References

Abdullah, M.K. and Mathew, R. (1965). *The Time of the Peacock*. North Ryde, NSW: Angus and Robertson.

Bosi, P. (1973). *Checkmate*. Sydney, NSW: Kurunda.

Bouras, G. (1986). *A Foreign Wife*. Melbourne: McPhee Gribble/Penguin.

Cusack, D. (1955). *The Sun in Exile*. Marlin.

Deszery, A. (1980). A Handful of Earth from Home. In *Neighbours*. Deszery Ethnic Publications.

Encarnação, J.J. (1979). *East Timor Poems*.

Foks, H. (1982). Ambitions, illusions and facts. In Gunew, S. (ed.), *Displacements*. Geelong, Vic.: Deakin University Press.

Hennessy, G. (1983). Mondays. *The Bulletin Literary Supplement*, 5 July.

Houbein, L. (1984). Survival Switch. In *Everything is Real*. Brisbane, Qd: Phoenix.

Houbein, L. (1988). *Walk a Barefoot Road*. Sydney, NSW: ABC.

Johnston, G. (1964). *My Brother Jack*. London: Collins.

Ker Wilson, B. (1984). *Jane Austen in Australia*. Richmond, Vic.: Heinemann Australia.

Loukakis, A. (1981). *For the Patriarch*. St Lucia, Qd: University of Queensland Press.

Lurie, M. (1982). *Flying Home*. Ringwood, Vic.: Penguin Australia.

Masters, O. (1982). *The Home Girls*. St Lucia, Qd: University of Queensland Press.

Masters, O. (1985). *A Long Time Dying*. St Lucia, Qd: University of Queensland Press.

Merritt, R. (1978). *The Cakeman*. Sydney, NSW: Currency Press.

Park, R. (1980) *Playing Beatie Bow*. Harmondsworth: Puffin.

Rooke, D. (1974). *Double Ex*. London: Gollancz.

Sharpe, M. (1983). *The Traeger Kid*. Chippendale, NSW: APCOL

Skrzynecki, P. (1975). *Immigrant Chronicle*. St Lucia, Qd: University of Queensland Press.

Skrzynecki, P. (1982). *The Polish Immigrant*. Brisbane, Qd: Phoenix.

Skrzynecki, P. (1987). *The Wild Dogs*. St Lucia, Qd: University of Queensland Press.

Skrzynecki, P. (1988). *Joseph's Coat*. Sydney, NSW: Hale and Iremonger.

Waten, J. (1969). *From Odessa to Odessa*. Cheshire.

Waten, J. (1978). *Love and Rebellion*. Melbourne, Vic.: Macmillan.

Wheatley, N. (1982). *Five Times Dizzy*. Melbourne, Vic.: Oxford.

Wheatley, N. (1984). *Dancing in the Anzac Dell*. Melbourne, Vic.: Oxford.

Zavos, S. (1983). Tales out of School. *The Bulletin* Literary Supplement, 5 July.

Books for use in the classroom

Rudine Sims Bishop (Chapter 2) suggests the following African-American children's books, published between 1981 and 1990. Because the choice is deliberately of recent titles, most have so far only been published in the USA. However, several of the writers – notably Pat Cummings, Rosa Guy, Virginia Hamilton and Mildred Taylor – are already well known in the UK and elsewhere:

Clifton, L. (1983). *Everett Anderson's Goodbye* (illustrated by A. Grifalconi). New York: Holt. In the last of the Everett Anderson books by the award-winning poet, Everett passes through the five stages of grief, mourning the death of his father. The fine pencil drawings reflect the emotional power of the brief poetic text.

Cummings, P. (1991). *Clean Your Room, Harvey Moon*. New York: Bradbury Press. Harvey Moon is made to clean his room on Saturday morning, when he would rather be watching his favourite cartoons. The results are less than perfect. Cummings' colourful and humorous drawings and verse depict a typical middle-class African-American child.

Greenfield, E. (1988). *Grandpa's Face* (illustrated by F. Cooper). New York: Philomel. Tamika and her actor grandfather have an especially warm relationship. When she sees him practising a hateful face in preparation for a play, she fears that one day he will look at her with no love in his eyes. He finds a way to reassure her. Intergenerational relationships and extended families are important themes in African-American children's literature.

Greenfield, E. (1989). *Nathaniel Talking* (illustrated by J.S. Gilchrist). New York: Black Butterfly. Eighteen poems in the voice of 9-year-old Nathaniel, an active spirited boy, thinking about his experiences, dreaming about his past and his future. Greenfield draws on black music, incorporating a rap and some blues. Lively black-and-white pencil drawings.

Guy, R. (1989). *The Ups and Downs of Carl Davis III*. New York: Delacorte. In an effort to shield him from the evils of the big city, Carl Davis III has been sent from New York to South Carolina to live with his grandmother. In a series of sometimes humorous letters home, Carl reports on his ups and downs – his efforts to enlighten the benighted southerners about Black history, his failed attempts to make friends, his gradual steps towards growing up.

Hamilton, V. (1985). *The People Could Fly: American Black Folktales* (illustrated by

L. Dillon and D. Dillon). New York: Knopf. A landmark collection of African-American folklore, illustrated by the Dillons' 40 striking black-and-white drawings. Includes tales representative of the spectrum of Black American folk stories.

Hamilton, V. (1986). *The Magical Adventures of Pretty Pearl.* New York: Harper. Hamilton weaves together African-American history, legend and myth in this fantasy novel featuring god child Pretty Pearl, sister to High John the Conquerer and John Henry. Pretty comes from Mount Kenya to the southern USA, joins a community of Free Blacks just after the Civil War, and makes a difficult choice. A complex, layered work.

Hamilton, V. (1990). *Cousins.* New York: Philomel. One of the premier writers of children's books explores the relationships within an African-American extended family. Cammy's beloved Gram Tut helps her to overcome the grief and depression brought on by the accidental death of one of her cousins.

Hansen, J. (1986). *Which Way Freedom?* New York: Walker. Historical fiction. Obi, a former slave, fights in the Civil War, and searches for freedom as he learns to survive in his new life.

Hansen, J. (1988). *Out From This Place.* New York: Walker. The sequel to *Which Way Freedom?* When Obi joined the war he had left Easter behind. This novel examines Easter's life during the Reconstruction Era after the Civil War. Together, these two books offer an African-American perspective on the black struggle for freedom in nineteenth-century USA.

Howard, E.F. (1991). *Aunt Flossie's Hats (and Crabcakes Later)* (illustrated by J. Ransome). New York: Clarion. Sarah and Susan delight in spending Sunday afternoons with great-great-aunt Flossie, who owns boxes and boxes of hats, and has a story to go with each hat. After stories comes the treat – a family trip to a restaurant for crabcakes. A middle-class black family sharing its history.

Johnson, A. (1989). *Tell Me a Story, Mama* (illustrated by D. Soman). New York: Orchard. A little girl wants her mother to tell a familiar story at bedtime. The ensuing dialogue demonstrates that the true story, from her mother's childhood, is indeed familiar. Who is telling the story anyway?

McKissack, P. (1986) *Flossie and the Fox* (illustrated by R. Isadora). New York: Dial. Flossie outsmarts a sly old fox and safely delivers the eggs to Miz Viola. Told in Southern Black vernacular, this story is in the tradition of African-American folk stories in which cleverness and a quick tongue are important survival tools.

Myers, W.D. (1988). *Fallen Angels,* New York: Scholastic. Richie Perry, a 17-year-old from Harlem, is sent to Vietnam. He experiences both the horrors of war and the camaraderie that grows among young men who share the boredom of the barracks and the fear of the trenches. Raises questions about the morality of war and its effects on the humanity of soldiers and civilians alike.

Myers, W.D. (1988). *Scorpions.* New York: Harper. Jamal and his best friend Tito struggle to survive on the mean city streets of Harlem. Jamal, in an effort to help his imprisoned brother, accepts a gun, which brings serious changes to his life. A compassionate exploration of a family's attempt to keep hope alive in an environment that seems hopeless.

Myers, W.D. (1990). *The Mouse Rap.* New York: Harper. A light and humorous look at a young teenage boy growing up in Harlem. The Mouse spends his summer involved in several ventures, including a search for hidden treasure in an abandoned house.

Ringgold, F. (1991). *Tar Beach*. New York: Cassie Louise Lightfoot is 8 years old, and she can fly! From the rooftop of her New York apartment building (Tar Beach), she imagines that she can fly over the city and make it her own. Developed from a story quilt, this picture book celebrates Cassie's determination as well as the power of imagination.

Tate, E. (1987). *The Secret of Gumbo Grove*. New York: Franklin Watts. Raisin, who is 11, causes a big stir when, in helping to clean up a cemetery, she uncovers the local African-American history many townspeople want to remain buried.

Taylor, M. (1987). *The Friendship*. New York: Dial. The Logan children from *Roll of Thunder* witness the attack on Mr Tom Bee, an old African-American man who refuses to address the storeowner, whom he had once befriended, as *Mister* John. Caught up in the overt racist atmosphere of 1930s Mississippi, John Wallace is unable to rise above it. In this 53-page book, the children see a courageous black man defiantly maintaining his dignity.

Taylor, M. (1990). *Mississippi Bridge*. New York: Dial. An ironic story, told by Jeremy Sims, the white boy who wishes so much to be a friend of the Logan children. Black passengers, including the Logan children's grandmother, are put off a bus to make room for late-arriving white passengers. A gut-wrenching surprise ending. Mississippi in the 1930s.

Walter, M.P. (1986). *Justin and the Best Biscuits in the World*. New York: Lothrop, Lee and Shepard. Justin has a hard time living in a home where he is the only male, and is expected to do 'women's work'. On a visit to his ranch, his grandfather helps him unlearn sexist stereotypes, and at the same time teaches him some African-American history.

Denise Newfield (Chapter 3) recommends these authors and/or anthologies as representative of South African literature today for students outside South Africa. In this case, most of the novelists and short story writers are published in the UK and elsewhere: drama and poetry will be more difficult to find. See Chapter 3 references above for publishers where available:

Fiction
Some of the authors mentioned have a large oeuvre from which additional titles could be selected:
Brink, A.: *A Dry White Season*.
Coetzee, J.M.: *Waiting for the Barbarians*.
Dikobe, M.: *The Marabi Dance*.
Gordimer, N.: *July's People*.
Lessing, D.: *The Grass is Singing*.
Paton, A.: *Cry, the Beloved Country*.
Plomer, W.: *Turbott Wolfe*.

Autobiographies
Khuzwayo, E.: *Call Me Woman*.
Mattera, D.: *Memory is the Weapon*.
Mphahlele, E. *Down Second Avenue*.
Mphahlele, E.: *Afrika, My Music*.

Short stories
The South African short story is a particularly accomplished and readable genre. Any collection by the following authors is recommended: H.C. Bosman, N. Gordimer, N. Nakasa (short journalistic pieces rather than stories), N. Ndebele, A. Paton, P. Smith and C. Themba.

The following anthologies of short stories are recommended for a broader spectrum:

Gray, S. (ed.) (1985). *The Penguin Book of South African Stories.* Harmondsworth: Penguin.

Marquard, J. (ed.) (1978). *A Century of South African Short Stories.* Johannesburg: A.D. Donker.

Drama
Works by the following dramatists or drama groups are integral to South African resistance culture; however, it must be stressed that much of the protest theatre of the last two decades has been workshop or community theatre that has not been finally scripted or published:

Athol Fugard; Junction Avenue Theatre Company; Matsemela Manaka; Maishe Maponya; P., Mtwa, M. Ngema and B. Simon (co-authors); Mbongeni Ngema; Barney Simon; Pieter-Dirk Uys; Workshop '71.

Short anthologies of plays:

Gray, S. (ed.) (1986). *Market Plays.* Johannesburg: A.D. Donker.

Hauptfleisch, Temple and Steadman (eds) (1984). *South African Theatre: Four Plays and an Introduction.* Pretoria: HAUM.

Kavanagh, R.M. (ed.) (1981). *South African People's Plays.* London: Heinemann.

Poetry
The following poets may be studied in relation to the theme of this book; however, mention must be made of the many unpublished oral protest poems chanted at political rallies, funerals and other community occasions: Roy Campbell, Jeremy Cronin, Mafika Gwala, Douglas Livingstone, James Matthews, Oswald Mtshali, Sipho Sepamla, Mongane Wally Serote and Christopher Van Wyk.

Two poetry collections are recommended for a broader spectrum:

Chapman, M. (ed.) (1981). *A Century of South African Poetry.* Johannesburg: A.D. Donker.

Couzens, T. and Patel, E. (eds) (1982). *The Return of the Amasi Bird: Black South African Poetry 1891–1981.* Johannesburg: Ravan Press.

Comics
The Storyteller Group (1991). *99 Sharp St: The River Of Our Dreams.* Johannesburg: A Storyteller Group Publication. Copies of this comic may be ordered from The Storyteller Group, 80 Richmond Avenue, Auckland Park, Johannesburg, South Africa.

Sibani Raychaudhuri (Chapter 6) gives these examples of literature from South Asia. Titles published by South Asian publishers are often available through specialist booksellers in and around the centres of cities:

Anand, M.R. (1935–40). *Untouchable, The Village, Across the Black Water* and *The*

Sword and the Sickle (London: Arnold/Heinemann). Mulk Raj Anand's writings are highly regarded for their themes of social protest and their literary quality. *Untouchable* is part of Anand's campaign against caste. His trilogy, the three last titles given above, tries to give a broad picture of the break-up of the old order based upon the traditional values of an agrarian society.

Ash, R. (ed.) (1980). *Short stories from India, Pakistan and Bangladesh*. London: Harrap. An anthology of 15 stories, translated from Urdu, Punjabi, Hindi, Gujerati and Malayalam. The authors represented range from the founding figures of modern literature to contemporary writers.

Bandyopadhyay, M. (1975). *Boatman of the Padma* (translated by H. Mukerjee). New Delhi: National Book Trust. A Bengali novel. The writer weaves round a boatman a simple tale that makes the reader sense vividly the life and loves of boatmen on the River Padma.

Banerji, B. (1986). *Pather Panchali* (translated by Clarke and Mukherji). London: Lokamaya Press. A Bengali novel. A most loved and famous story – basis of Satyajit Ray's film – about growing up in a Bengali village at the end of the nineteenth century. The novel paints a picture of rural Bengal through the eyes of a 10-year-old boy, Apu, and his sister, Durga.

Contractor, C. (1989). *An Introduction to Indo-British and South Asian Literature for Teachers in Secondary Schools and Colleges*, 3rd edn. The Publications Department, Multi-cultural Education Centre, Bishop Road, Bishopston, Bristol, Avon BS7 8LS, UK.

Chowdury, K. (ed. and translator) (1977). *Fifty Poems from Bangladesh*. Calcutta: United Writers.

Desai, A. (1979). *The Peacock Garden*. London: Heinemann. A story of a Muslim girl and her family hiding in an enclosed mosque garden with peacocks, in order to escape from the violence of partition in India.

Desai, A. (1981). *Fire on the Mountain*. Harmondsworth: Penguin. A beautifully composed, deep and sensitive novel which tells the story of a young child, Raka, who goes to stay with her great-grandmother at a mountain resort in the hills of North India.

Desai, A. (1983). *The Village by the Sea*. London: Heinemann/Harmondsworth: Penguin. A story of two rural children, concerned about the proposed development of their village into an overspill township for Bombay.

Dhingra, L. (1988). *Amritvela*. London: The Women's Press. A novel which presents a search for identity within a story written with humour and sensitivity.

Hossain, A. (1988). *Sunlight on a Broken Column*. London: Arnold/Heinemann. An autobiographical novel. The author, as Laila, grows up in semi-purdah in a well-to-do household in India in the 1930s.

Jussawalla, A. (ed.) (1974). *New Writing in India*. Harmondsworth: Penguin. A collection of articles, plays, extracts from novels and poems by young writers.

Nandy, P. (ed.) *The Voice of a Nation: Poems from Bangladesh*.

Narayan, R.K. (1980). *Swami and Friends*. Oxford: Oxford University Press. An account of a 10-year-old boy's adventures in Narayan's imaginary town of Malgudi in the 1930s.

Rao, R. (1974). *Kanthapura*, 2nd edn. Madras: Oxford University Press. The story, told by an old woman, of a small village in southern India, is about the gradual changes that the Gandhian movement made to that village.

Tagore, R. (1945). *My Boyhood Days* (translated by M. Sykes). Calcutta: Viswa Bharati. Tagore's short autobiography.

Tagore, R. (1988). *This World is Beautiful.* The Tagore Centre, Alexandra Park Library, Alexandra Park Road, London N22 4UJ, UK. Rabindranath Tagore in translation in a collection for young people.

Tagore, R. (1985). *Selected Poems* (translated by W. Radice). Harmondsworth: Penguin. Tagore was an outstanding poet and is universally recognized as the major classic writer of Bengal. William Radice's selection provides an appraisal of his poetry.

Welch, J. (ed.) (1988). *Stories from South Asia.* Oxford: Oxford University Press. This collection provides an exciting and stimulating introduction to the literature of South Asia and is particularly suitable for English and Literature courses.

Emrys Evans (Chapter 10) used six novels as starters, after which a number of individual students read a variety of related books on their own. Some short stories were also used during the lessons together. The books we started with were as follows (note that the dates given are those of first publication and the publishers are those of paperback editions):

From South Africa
Brink, A. (1979). *A Dry White Season.* London: Collins Flamingo/New York: Penguin.
Coetzee, J.M. (1983). *The Life and Times of Michael K.* Harmondsworth: Penguin.

From India
Jhabvala, R.P. (1960). *The Householder.* Harmondsworth: Penguin/New York: Norton.

From the USA
Morrison, T. (1987). *Beloved.* London: Chatto and Windus, Pan-Picador/New York: New American Library.

From the Caribbean
Naipaul, V.S. (1959). *Miguel Street.* Harmondsworth: Penguin.

From East Africa
Wa Thiong'o Ngũgĩ (1965). *The River Between.* London: Heinemann (African Writers Series).

Other books that students read
Achebe, C. (1958). *Things Fall Apart*; (1960). *No Longer at Ease*; (1964). *Arrow of God.* These three titles are published in the UK in one volume as *The African Trilogy* (London: Pan Books, 1988). In the USA, the first two titles are published in New York by Fawcett, the third by Doubleday.
Anthony, M. (1983). *Green Days by the River.* London: Heinemann (Caribbean Writers Series).

Brink, A. (1967). *The Ambassador*. London: Collins Flamingo/New York: Summit Books.

Brink, A. (1976). *An Instant in the Wind*. London: Collins Flamingo/New York: Penguin.

Coetzee, J.M. (1980). *Waiting for the Barbarians*. Harmondsworth: Penguin.

Jhabvala, R.P. (1975). *Heat and Dust*. London: Macdonald-Futura/New York: Simon and Schuster.

Morrison, T. (1970). *The Bluest Eye*. London: Collins Triad-Crafton/New York: Washington Square Press.

Morrison, T. (1973). *Sula*. London: Collins Triad-Crafton/New York: New American Library.

Morrison, T. (1978). *Song of Solomon*. London: Pan-Picador/New York: New American Library.

Morrison, T. (1981). *Tar Baby*. London: Collins Triad-Grafton/New York: New American Library.

Ngũgĩ Wa Thiong'o (1964). *Weep Not, Child*. London: Heinemann (African Writers Series).

Ngũgĩ Wa Thiong'o (1977). *Petals of Blood*. London: Heinemann (African Writers Series).

Short stories read aloud to the class

La Cuma, A. (1968). 'The Lemon Orchard' and other shorter tales from *A Walk in the Night*. London: Heinemann (African Writers Series)/Evanston, Ill.: Northwestern University Press.

Narayan, R.K. (1982). 'Iswaran' and 'The Doctor's Word' from *Malgudi Days*. Harmondsworth: Penguin.

Ray, S. (1987). 'Khagam' and 'Night of the Indigo' from *Stories*. Harmondsworth: Penguin.

Jim Kable (Chapter 11) recommends a number of anthologies, picture books, poems, dramatic texts, short stories and novels on immigrant cultures in Australia. Many of these are published by small publishing houses in Australia and are not easily available elsewhere. A letter direct to the publishers or an Australian bookseller such as Glee Books, Glebe Point Road, Sydney, NSW would be needed from outside Australia:

Anthologies

Davis, J., Muecke, S., Narogin, M. and Shoemaker, A. (eds) (1990). *Paperbark*: A collection of black Australian writing. St Lucia, Qd: University of Queensland Press. Thirty-six Aboriginal and Islander authors from all parts of Australia are included, their work ranging across time and genres, from the 1840s to the present, from transcriptions of oral literature to rock opera. Prose, poetry, song, drama and polemic are presented with passion and power.

Gunew, S. and Mahyuddin, J. (eds) (1988). *Beyond the Echo*. St Lucia, Qd: University of Queensland Press. Forty-eight women writers of non Anglo-Celtic background paint the complexity of life in a culturally diverse Australia. This collection addresses the invisibility of the lives of women of many contemporary depictions of Australian society.

Hammer, G. (comp.) (1988). *Pomegranates*. Newtown: Millenium Books. From the 1890s to 1980s, this collection uncovers a century of Jewish Australian writing. Historically valuable, treats issues known and experienced by all immigrant and cultural minorities. Over 50 writers demonstrate the vital part played by writers of Jewish origin in Australia's literary life.

Holt, R.F. (ed.) (1983). *The Strength of Tradition*. St Lucia, Qd: University of Queensland Press. A collection of stories which explore the issues faced by immigrants and by the children of immigrants. Writers of Anglo–Australian background observe their fellow Australians of other ethnic origins.

Jurgensen, M. (ed.) (1981). *Ethnic Australia*. Brisbane, Qd: Phoenix. An important collection of literary pieces written by authors from a wide variety of immigrant backgrounds. Responses to the immigrant experience.

Kable, J. (ed.) (1990). *Made in Australia*. Melbourne, Vic.: Oxford University Press. Anthology of short writing uncovering the cultural and ethnic diversity at the heart of the Australian identity. Sixty-eight writers add insights into issues ranging from origins, homesickness, cultural pathways, names, language and issue of race. Suggested classroom activities to follow up issues raised.

Kable, J. (ed.) (1990). *An Arc of Australian Voices*. Melbourne, Vic.: Oxford University Press. Companion volume to *Made in Australia*. Longer pieces of writing from print media, novel extracts, short stories, autobiographical writing, all selected to reveal the diversity of Australia's cultural life.

Kanarakis, G. (1987). *Greek Voices in Australia*. Canberra: ANU Press. Eighty-two Greek writers in Australia, their biographies and selections of their writing (translated from Greek, where necessary) demonstrate the riches of the literary heritage brought to Australia from the Greek-speaking world. New insights into the Hellenic cultural presence in Australia.

Loh, M. (ed.) (1980). *With Courage in Their Cases*. Coburg, Vic.: FILEF. Thirty-five Italian workers, immigrants to Australia between 1920 and 1980, explain their various experiences in coping with prejudice, the English language and family separation as they established themselves in Australia.

Lowenstein, W. and Loh, M. (1977). *The Immigrants*. Hyland House. Oral history at its best. A landmark publication in which 17 immigrants to Australia between the years 1890 and 1970 tell their stories.

Skrzynecki, P. (ed.) (1985). *Joseph's Coat*. Hale and Iremonger. Writers are of non-English speaking origin. This literature deals with aspects of life which are not always perceived as being mainstream. Black Australian voices highlight this collection.

Picture books

Crofts, P. (comp.) (1987). *Warnayarra – The Rainbow Snake* by The Senior Boys Class, Lajamanu School. Ashton Scholastic. A true story, naively told. A powerful truth is often best dealt with thus. A story told by students from a remote community in the Northern Territory.

Loh, M. and Rawlins, D. (1985). *The Kinder Hat*. Ashton Scholastic. Children's picture books may be read on many levels. This story says most in the brilliant artwork. Which languages and cultures are represented by the posters on the wall, by the names of the characters, by the images on the street and in the house? Much to say about contemporary, multicultural Australia.

Torres, P. and Williams, M. (1987). *The Story of Crow*. Broome: Magabala Books. An exciting bilingual book, it clearly demonstrates for all readers that English is not the only language spoken or read by Australians. Brilliantly illustrated, this traditional tale, like all good literature, has a moral too.

Wheatley, N. and Rawlins, D. (1987). *My Place*. Collins Dove. Moving from Australia's bicentennial year in 1988 to 1788, the history of a Sydney street is peeled back, and seen through the eyes of a variety of children living in one of the houses. The map of the area, the social and historical concerns of the neighbourhood reveal in decade slices the everchanging ethnic fabric representative of the nation at large. Like bookends, the families present in the house or at its site in 1988 and 1788 are Koori.

Poetry

Brett, L. (1986). *The Auschwitz Poems*. Scribe, Brunswick. The children of those who survived do not necessarily escape scot free. Poems, spare narrow slivers of words symbolic of so much, are matched by bleak charcoal sketches done by the poet's husband, David Rankin. A testament to courage and endurance and a reminder of the dreadful inhumanity periodically unleashed upon those made scapegoats.

Noffs, T. (1983). *Childhood Memories of Henry Lawson Country* and *Henry Lawson's Mudgee Poems*. Darlinghurst: The Wayside Foundation. A much-loved Christian, Ted Noffs reflects on his ancestors, the German settlers of Eurunderee in the Mudgee district where he was born, and where he spent his school holidays. But it was the same district and the same people immortalized by the writing of Henry Lawson, son of a Norwegian immigrant to Australia, who also grew up here. This collection reminds us that Australia has always been an immigrant nation.

Skrzynecki, P. (1982). *The Polish Immigrant*. Brisbane, Qd: Phoenix. Poems which cover the journey, both physical and spiritual, undertaken by immigrants. The poet embarks, arrives, matures, observes, commemorates, farewells and reflects on the gamut of life's experiences which are suffused by the added dimension of cultural differences from the mainstream.

Vleeskens, C. (1984). *The Day, The River*. St Lucia, Qd: University of Queensland Press. From the memories of the Old Holland to the reality of the New Holland, the poet draws a shadow across the journey, natural to one who makes the passage when a child. Gently insightful.

Drama

Summons, J. (1989). *Kamikaze Kate (and the Sword of Captain Kuroda)*. Paddington, NSW: Currency. This is a short play, but one which junior secondary students will enjoy both for the issues it raises to do with war as well as for its vigorous sense of humour. It makes pointed reference to the Pacific war and its pain, and this connection between Australia and Japan is timely when ghosts still remain to be exorcised.

Short stories

Brett, L. (1990). *Things Could be Worse*. Meanjin/MUP. These stories capture much that is true of those who have survived the holocaust. But it is the way the writer leavens with humour and with sympathetic insight the lives of human spirits warped by this most frightful of experiences that gives it enormous power. Will become a classic.

Giles, Z. (1989). *Miracle of the Waters*. Harmondsworth: Penguin. This is a group of stories linked by characters of diverse cultural backgrounds who travel to Moree, 700 km from Sydney, in order to take the healing waters of the mineral springs located there. Their individual tales are like parts of a mosaic which all together reveal contemporary Australia.

Shearston, T. (1979). *Something in the Blood*. St Lucia, Qd: University of Queensland Press. Stories set in Papua New Guinea before 1974 when Australia played at colonialist power. This collection exposes the process of colonialism and shows what it meant to be a white 'masta'. A jolt to the apathy of those who imagine they wouldn't or couldn't oppress.

Waten, J. (1978). *Love and Rebellion*. Melbourne, Vic.: Macmillan. Stories based on the life of a man who participated actively in the social issues of his time. One of the first writers to confront the alienation and discrimination suffered by immigrants to Australia, this collection tells us about the formative influences in his life.

Novels

Bandler, F. (1984). *Welou, My Brother*. Wild and Woolley. The author is descended from Pacific Islanders brought against their will in the latter part of the nineteenth century to work as slaves on sugar plantations in northern Australia. This story is based on experiences from that background. Another twist to the Australian story.

Kefala, A. (1984). *Alexia – A Tale of Two Cultures*. Sydney, NSW: John Ferguson. From the Old World to the New, this tale Emphasizes the Cultural Adjustment which has to be endured by making Generous use of Capital Letters. It reads like a fairly tale but there is no 'happy ever after'. Nevertheless, we do discover how it came to be that Alexia goes to university. Though set in New Zealand, there are only two or three references which establish this. Everything else is Australia of the 1950s, including obligatory false teeth, mowing lawns, and the public segregation of men and women.

Kelly, G. (1981). *Always Afternoon*. Collins. Shameful incidents from the history of Australia include the internment of those deemed enemy aliens in wartime. During the First World War, Trial Bay Gaol outside Kempsey in NSW became 'home' to Australian Germans, Germans who were Buddhist priests from Ceylon, missionaries from New Guinea and China, as well as those Germans of military personnel one might expect to be so imprisoned. A moving story based on history.

Lewitt, M. (1985). *No Snow in December*. Richmond, Vic.: Heinemann. Sequel to *Come Spring*, which tells of survival from the Nazis in Poland while hidden in a cellar by relatives on her Catholic mother's side of the family, this tale deals with the arrival and adjustments to life in Australia.

Sakkas, J. (1988). *Ilias*. Allen and Unwin. Images of Australia from the late 1920s through to the 1950s as the reader follows the fortunes of Ilias, emigrant from a small Greek island to Australia. The vicissitudes of life during the Depression, the experiences suffered during the War and beyond, and the increasing disillusion as dreams are not fulfilled are the real drama of life, believable and sad.

Sharpe, M. (1983). *The Traeger Kid.* Chippendale: APCOL. Trisha, a little Aranda girl living in Alice Springs, is the central character in this story written by a sociolinguist. Issues dealt with involve the use of languages other than English, traditional homelands, family relationships and the sorts of school experiences which will best allow young people to be successful, no matter what the cultural background.

Tomasetti, G. (1976). *Thoroughly Decent People.* McPhee Gribble. This book began as an MA thesis on folklore in Australia. Set in the centenary year of 1934 in Melbourne, it makes intelligible Anglo-Australian traditions. No publisher, unfortunately, acted upon her wish that it be translated into Greek during the 1970s for the benefit of the city's Greek community (third largest Greek-born community in the world after Athens and Salonika) so that they might better understand their new home.

Biographies/autobiographies

Bouras, G. (1986). *A Foreign Wife.* McPhee Gribble/Penguin. The author left comfortable middle-class Melbourne for an extended stay with her husband and two children in the Greek village of his birth. Six years later, she was still there, using writing as her means for coping with the enormous cultural and linguistic adjustments with which she was confronted. Anglo-Australians will easily identify with her situation; other immigrant Australians will recognize themselves in her experiences.

Edwards, C. and Read, P. (1989). *The Lost Children.* Doubleday. Thirteen Koori Australians from NSW tell about how they were taken as children from their families and of their struggles later on to find their natural parents. These are people who suffered under the same sorts of policies as Sally Morgan's family in Western Australia. The book is dedicated to all our Old People who never saw their children again and to all our children who never came home.

Houbein, L. (1990). *Wrong Face in the Mirror.* St Lucia, Qd: University of Queensland Press. From Holland where she was a child through the Second World War, to Australia and periods in Papua New Guinea and South-East Asia, the author traces her life along a line of ethnicity and the questions posed by a world in which, surely, all people are related. While the impetus springs from her childhood and immediate family, this life has flowered in its Australian setting.

Morgan, S. (1989). *My Place.* Fremantle, WA: Fremantle Arts Centre Press. The most powerful voice in Australia, Sally Morgan's quest for a cultural and ethnic identity is told in this detective story. To know her true place in this country she had to lay bare her Aboriginal family's past, revealing another ugly chapter from Australia's social history. Her great uncle, her mother and finally her grandmother succumb to her persistence and tell their stories. Moving, healing.

The teachers' bookshelf

The following suggestions are for further reading in any school, college or department which wants to use a variety of texts for reading against racism. They offer both ideas for more material, and for pedagogical approaches in the classroom. They have been compiled by the editor, with the considerable and valued assistance of Margaret M. Robbins, lecturer at Birmingham Polytechnic:

ATCAL (1988). *Reading Guides: African, Caribbean and Indo-British Literature for the Classroom.* London: ILEA English Centre (now available from NATE Birley School Annexe, Fox Lane Site, Frechville, Sheffield S12 4WY, UK).

Chinweizu (1988). *Voices from Twentieth Century Africa: Griots and Towncriers.* London: Faber and Faber.

Cook, D. (1977). *African Literature: A Critical View.* London: Longman.

Dabydeen, D. (ed.) (1985). *The Black Presence in English Literature.* Manchester: Manchester University Press.

Dabydeen, D. (ed.) (1988). *A Handbook for Teaching Caribbean Literature.* London: Heinemann.

Dabydeen, D. and Wilson-Tagoe, N. (1988). *A Reader's Guide to West Indian and Black British Literature.* London: Hansib/Rutherford.

Dixon, B. (1977). *Catching them Young: 1. Sex, Race and Class in Children's Fiction.* London: Pluto Press.

Elkin, J. and Triggs, P. (1985). *The 'Books for Keeps' Guide to Children's Books for a Multicultural Society 8–12.* London: School Bookshop Association.

Evans, M. (ed.) (1983). *Black Women Writers.* London: Pluto Press.

Gunner, E. (1984). *A Handbook for Teaching African Literature.* London: Heinemann.

Guptara, P. (1986). *Black British Literature.* Coventry: Dangaroo Press.

Klein, G. (1985). *Reading into Racism: Bias in Children's Literature and Learning Materials.* London: Routledge.

Miller, J. (1983). *Many Voices: Bilingualism, Culture and Education.* London: Routledge and Kegan Paul.

Ngũgĩ Wa Thiong'o (1972). *Homecoming: Essays on African and Caribbean Literature, Culture and Politics.* London: Heinemann.

Ngũgĩ Wa Thiong'o (1986). *Decolonising the Mind: The Politics of Language in African Literature.* London: James Currey/Heinemann.

Ogungbesan, K. (ed.) (1979). *New West African Literature*. London: Heinemann.

Palmer, E. (1972). *An Introduction to the African Novel*. London: Heinemann.

Ramchand, K. (1976). *An Introduction to the Study of West African Literature*. London: Nelson.

Russell, S. (ed.) (1990). *Render Me My Song: African American Women Writers from Slavery to the Present*. London: Pandora Press.

Scafe, S. (1989). *Teaching Black Literature*. London: Virago.

Schipper, M. (ed.) (1985). *Unheard Words: Women and Literature in Africa, the Arab World, Asia, the Caribbean and Latin America*. London: Allison and Busby.

Shava, P.V. (1989). *A People's Voice: Black South African Writing in the Twentieth Century*. London: Zed Books.

Soyinka, W. (1976). *Myth, Literature and the African World*. Cambridge: Cambridge University Press.

Walder, D. (1990). *Literature in the Modern World: Critical Essays and Documents*. Oxford: Oxford University Press.

Whitehead, W. (1988). *Different Faces: Growing up with Books in a Multicultural Society*. London: Pluto Press.

Young, A.V. (1987). *The Image of Black Women in 20th Century South American Poetry: A Bilingual Anthology*. Washington DC: Three Continents Press Inc.

Zimet, S.G. (1976). *Print and Prejudice*. London: Hodder and Stoughton.

The Journal *Wasafiri*. Perspectives on African, Caribbean, Asian and Black British literature, published twice yearly by ATCAL (Association for the Teaching of Caribbean, African, Asian and Associated Literature).

Index